Praise for **Jesus, Beginnings,**

"Jesus, Beginnings, and Science: A Guide for Group Conversation is a rich resource that sheds light into the topics of creation, human origin, and limits of human knowledge.... It is a timely, invaluable guide."

—**Louise Ko Huang, Ph.D., Director, Center for Research in Science, Azusa Pacific University**

"[This] guide is immensely practical and will enable anyone, regardless of their background in science or religion, to lead effective and cordial conversations about some of the most divisive topics of our day. Highly recommended."

—**Karl Giberson, Professor of Science & Religion at Stonehill College and author of**
Saving Darwin: How to Be a Christian and Believe in Evolution

"[This book] is perfect for small groups of interested students. The basic message is that Christianity and science are compatible. I recommend the Guide with great enthusiasm."

—**Stephen T. Davis, Russell K. Pitzer Professor of Philosophy, Claremont McKenna College**

"This study guide... offers a series of skillfully crafted group discussion experiences that participants will find engaging, eye-opening, and non-threatening, whatever commitments on religion and science they bring with them."

—**Rev. Dr. Christopher R. Smith, author of the** *Understanding the Books of the Bible*
study guide series and the blog *Good Question*

"I believe this will be a most helpful new approach to an ever present struggle. I wish I had this as a college student wrestling with issues of science and my faith."

—**Terry Morrison, PhD, Emeritus Director, Faculty Ministry, InterVarsity Christian Fellowship**

"I enthusiastically recommend this winsome and intelligent guide to this important subject for all Christians—especially those who feel that their faith is challenged by science."

—**Tremper Longman III, Distinguished Scholar of Biblical Studies, Westmont College**

"With helpful overviews, engaging questions, and thoughtful reflections, the Vosburgs help readers study the Scriptures themselves and draw their own conclusions without endorsing one view over another. I highly recommend *Jesus, Beginnings, and Science* for use by churches and campus ministries in small group contexts."

—**Dr. Stan Wallace, President and CEO of Global Scholars and**
co-editor of *Science: Christian Perspectives for the New Millennium*

"This is a fantastic resource to bridge the chasm between science and faith that strands so many to agnosticism or outright rejection of God's truth."

—Dr. Dean N. Smith, Pastor, The Highway Community and President, Highway Media, Executive Producer of *From the Dust: Conversations in Creation*

"I know of no finer introductory-level study guide for the discussion and biblical study of the most perplexing issues at the interface between science and Christian faith."

—Darrel R. Falk, Professor of Biology, Emeritus, Point Loma Nazarene University; Senior Advisor for Dialog and Former President, BioLogos

"David and Kate Vosburg have done an amazing job of opening up dialogue on this topic and providing a road map for those who believe that God speaks through both His creation and His Word."

—Glenn Gunderson, Lead Pastor, Purpose Church, Pomona, California

"This wonderful resource blends humble scholarly insight with compassionate pastoral care. I wish someone could have guided me through this material when I was starting college."

—Justin L. Barrett, Ph.D., Chief Project Developer, Office for Science, Theology, and Religion Initiatives, Fuller Theological Seminary

"This is a wonderfully creative way of studying God's creation through the whole of the Bible and opens up fresh ways of understanding that will delight and inspire—yet another example of the historic friendship between science and faith."

—Denis Alexander, Emeritus Director, The Faraday Institute for Science and Religion, St. Edmund's College, Cambridge.

"This is a beautiful group study and discussion guide on science for all Christians, interweaving awe of Creation, love for Jesus, understanding of science, humility toward Scripture, and respect for fellow believers with different views about science and faith."

—Dr. Jennifer Wiseman, astronomer, author, and speaker

"The Vosburgs have given us a valuable introduction to the subject, both friendly and helpful. This study isn't here to settle every controversial question, but it certainly presents an orientation that is trusting toward the Bible, positive toward the sciences, and charitable toward other Christians."

—C. John ("Jack") Collins, PhD, Professor of Old Testament, Covenant Theological Seminary

Read more reviews at PierPress.com

Jesus, Beginnings, and Science

A GUIDE FOR GROUP CONVERSATION

BY DAVID A. VOSBURG, PhD
AND KATE VOSBURG

Pier Press® Farmville, VA

Pier Press, LLC
P.O. Box 366
Farmville, VA 23901
PierPress.com

ISBN 978-0-9969915-1-3 (pbk)

ISBN 978-0-9969915-2-0 (ebook)

Library of Congress Control Number: 2017949988

Cover and interior design by Buffy Bellenir • www.buffybellenir.com

Contents

PART THREE
What does the Bible say about science?

CLOSING REMARKS

INTRODUCTION

Finding Jesus

Ellen, a sophomore taking my chemistry course, was standing at my office door. "Professor Vosburg," she said, "I saw your blog posts on science and Christianity. Can we talk about them?" That began a series of conversations with Ellen about faith, and then one of Ellen's friends started meeting with her to guide her in looking more closely at the Bible. Seven months later, Ellen accepted Jesus.

Sam was also a college sophomore, and he attended a lecture I gave on science and Christianity. He was shocked to learn that scientists could be Christians and that some of them were actually people he knew! He was already committed to becoming a scientist, but once he realized that scientists could embrace faith and follow Jesus, he reconsidered his atheism. After several talks with me, Sam joined a dorm Bible study for seekers. A year later, he became a Christian and was baptized on Easter Sunday.

Both Ellen and Sam thought that a person couldn't believe in Jesus and science at the same time. When they heard otherwise, they wanted to see what the Bible really said, to explore ideas with peers, and to see what options were open to them.

Exploring and understanding the relationship between faith and science is very important—and not just for prospective scientists. Ellen and Sam thought Christianity and science were incompatible because that was the impression they got from Christians around them. Equally at fault were non-Christians who insisted that God and science don't mix.

How can Christians and non-Christians engage with faith and science productively? We must have honest and open dialogue, take both the Bible and science seriously, and convey respect for others—even when we disagree with their views. I hope this guide will catalyze good and healthy conversations for believers and for seekers.

To spark such discussions, this guide for groups examines a series of passages from Scripture that offer perspectives on God's creation, human origins, and science. Some of these passages are poetic, and some have more of a narrative structure. Many describe God's majesty and can inspire wonder and awe in us. Alongside the Bible studies, the sessions invite participants to engage common questions about the Bible and science. At the end of the guide, discussion leaders and others who wish to explore topics more deeply will find notes and suggested additional resources. This guide is appropriate for use in existing small groups or for new groups gathered specifically to discuss the Bible and science.

All Scripture quotations from the New Testament (originally in Greek) use the New International Version (NIV); those from the Old Testament (originally in Hebrew) use the New Living Translation (NLT).

Words of Encouragement

From David A. Vosburg, PhD, Chemistry Professor

I wish I had been able to have good, healthy conversations about the integration of science and Christianity when I was in college. I hope this discussion guide stimulates many mature, gracious conversations and leads us from fear into dialogue and greater confidence in our faith. Finding such dialogue has been life-giving to me, increasing my awe of God's creation and bringing a deeper resonance between my faith in Jesus and my appreciation for science.

We need to have a greater understanding about how the Bible can relate to science and more respect for others' views, especially those views that differ from our own. This is important for unity within the church, for preserving the faith of young Christians when they learn more about science, and for presenting a more coherent and compelling gospel to people considering Christianity.

My experience in having conversations with other Christians about science and faith is that their concerns are more often about biblical authority than they are about science—that is why this guide focuses more on the Bible than on science. If this guide is used in a group setting, try to cultivate a culture of grace in community. None of us has it all figured out, but the groups we create can be welcoming places to think and talk about questions together. Such a group attitude can then be a model for having positive discussions on other controversial topics that relate to our Christian faith.

In Christ all things hold together.

David A. Vosburg, 2017

From Kate Vosburg, Pastor

I am not a scientist. I'm a college pastor. I remember being defensive when questions of science and faith came up in conversations in high school and college. I saw science as a threat to my faith in some areas, and I didn't know how to resolve those tensions because I didn't hear older Christians grappling with them. The people I did hear were as defensive and threatened as I was. That is, until I started talking with my college pastor about some of the questions. He didn't seem threatened by science. Talking with him and seeing his confidence in Christ and Scripture as he considered science gave me a new posture and hope in engaging my questions.

Years later, after reading Christian books, attending Christian lectures, and talking with Christians of various persuasions, I have come to appreciate science as a way to understand God's creation that increases my wonder of God. My confidence in the Bible as God's Word has increased. I am no longer defensive or tense when questions of science and faith arise.

This is what I hope to lead Christian college students to as many of them grapple with similar questions and tensions. I know the difference it made for me to talk openly with other Christians without fear of judgment. I long for God to strengthen their faith like God has strengthened mine.

As my Christian students and I come to peace with questions of science and faith, we've been able to share Jesus with seekers who are asking questions of science and faith. Ellen and Sam, David's two chemistry students, joined my Christian college group, and we helped them accept Jesus as Savior and Lord. As Christians reconciled with science, we were able to help non-Christians be reconciled with Christ. I pray that the Lord helps you through these Bible studies so you can do this as well.

To God be the glory.
Kate Vosburg, 2017

Suggestions
for Group Leaders

As leader of a discussion group, you do not need expert biblical knowledge or training as a teacher. Your job is simply to guide the group through each study, to allow members to make discoveries for themselves as they reflect on Bible passages, and to facilitate discussion so that everyone can participate. This guide may be used with students, churches, or home groups. Each session is designed to take 45–60 minutes with opportunities for reflection activities between meetings.

Preparing for meetings

Pray for God to bless your preparation and the members of the group. Read the session. Read and reread the Bible passage(s) and take notes, using colored pens or pencils to highlight repeated words, themes, or connections in the passage. Write down your own responses to the discussion questions that follow the text. Decide whether or not you would like to incorporate singing or music into your meeting; if so, select one or more of the suggested songs for that session or another of your own choosing. Be sure that every group member has a study guide, or at least easy access to the Bible passage(s) for the day.

Leading meetings

Choose a welcoming space for your meetings. At the first meeting, agree on a set of group expectations, such as these:

- Stay on topic.
- Let everyone participate fully.
- Listen respectfully when others are speaking.
- It is okay if not everyone else in the group agrees with you.

- Treat each other with grace and humility.
- Consider what is shared at the meetings to be confidential unless otherwise specified.

At the beginning of each meeting, ask the opening question and encourage all people present to share their responses. This allows all participants to speak and will encourage quieter members to contribute later.

To set the context for the session, ask a group member to read the paragraphs that follow the opening question. Invite another member to pray for the group, asking the Holy Spirit to give each member insight and understanding. Read the Bible passage(s) aloud; for some sessions, specific suggestions for assigning reading parts are given. After reading aloud, be sure everyone has time to quietly re-read the passages and to take notes before breaking into small groups for the discussion questions.

Once the small groups have had a chance to discuss the questions, regather everyone into a single group and invite several people to share highlights from their small-group conversations. If time permits, you may wish to read aloud "A Scientist's Reflection" and discuss it as a group. These commentaries offer insights based on David's perspective as a Christian who works as a researcher and teacher in science. Pray as suggested at the end of the session, supplementing with important ideas or concerns that arose from the large group conversation. Encourage group members to complete the "Reflect" section before your next meeting and to share what they learned with the group at the beginning of the next meeting.

Part One

What does the Bible say about creation?

Many people consider only Genesis 1–2 when they think about the Bible and creation. While the creation accounts in Genesis 1 and Genesis 2 are certainly important, they represent a small portion of the biblical message of creation. For example, there are a multitude of descriptions of creation in Psalms 8, 19, 33, 74, 104, and 148. God's dialogue with Job is especially rich in this regard. In fact, in his book *Faith & Wisdom in Science*, Christian physicist Tom McLeish proclaims Job 38–41 to be the most insightful biblical text on creation and science.

Biblical scholar William P. Brown also urges us to look beyond Genesis. In *The Seven Pillars of Creation*, Brown examines seven traditions or ways of creation in the Old Testament: Genesis 1:1–2:3, Genesis 2:4b–3:24, Job 38–41, Psalm 104, Proverbs 8:22–31, Ecclesiastes 1:2–11 and 12:1–7, and Isaiah 40–55. Just as we would hardly consider ignoring any of the four gospels (Matthew, Mark, Luke, and John) in learning about Jesus, Brown argues that we should not dismiss any of the "seven pillars of creation" if we wish to have a fuller understanding of God's creation. Two additional Old Testament passages describing God's creation are Proverbs 3:19–20 and Isaiah 65:17–25. Clearly there is far more to be found in the Bible about creation than just the first two chapters of Genesis!

The New Testament also offers many voices on creation in John (1:1–10 and 17:24), Acts (17:24–28), Romans (8:18–25),

I Corinthians (8:6), Colossians (1:15–17), Hebrews (1:2–3), I Peter (1:20), and 2 Peter (3:3–16), as well as the new creation in Revelation (21–22). While there are a wide variety of emphases and writing styles in all of these Old and New Testament passages, they are unified in asserting God as creator. Any biblical theology of creation needs to consider these as well as the Genesis accounts. Several helpful commentaries on creation passages in Scripture can be found at the end of this book in the Additional Resources section.

The four Bible studies in this part of the book will explore several different scriptural perspectives on creation from both the Old and New Testaments, and other passages will be considered in later sections. Be prepared to encounter the texts with fresh eyes and to learn something new!

CHAPTER 1

Jesus and Creation

OPENING QUESTION:

When you think of God's creation,
what words or images come to mind?

Jesus is the central and defining figure of Christianity. But does Jesus have anything to do with science and creation? Surprisingly, several New Testament passages speak to this, including the three passages from the gospel of John and the books of Colossians and Hebrews that are presented here.

John is one of Jesus' biographies, written to help people know Jesus as God's Son, not just a man. Here Jesus is called "the Word." Colossians is a letter from Paul, an early church leader, to Christians living in Colossae to help them follow Jesus. Hebrews is a more general letter written to encourage Jewish Christians to hold onto their faith in Christ. In both letters, Jesus is called "the Son."

PRAY as a group that the Holy Spirit would give each of you insight and understanding.

READ these three passages aloud together, with a different reader for each one.

John 1:1–5 (NIV)

¹ In the beginning was the Word, and the Word was with God, and the Word was God. ² He was with God in the beginning. ³ Through him all things were made; without him nothing was made that has been made. ⁴ In him was life, and that life was the light of all mankind. ⁵ The light shines in the darkness, and the darkness has not overcome it.

Colossians 1:15–17 (NIV)

15 The Son is the image of the invisible God, the firstborn over all creation. 16 For in him all things were created: things in heaven and on earth, visible and invisible, whether thrones or powers or rulers or authorities; all things have been created through him and for him. 17 He is before all things, and in him all things hold together.

Hebrews 1:1–3a (NIV)

1 In the past God spoke to our ancestors through the prophets at many times and in various ways, 2 but in these last days he has spoken to us by his Son, whom he appointed heir of all things, and through whom also he made the universe. 3 The Son is the radiance of God's glory and the exact representation of his being, sustaining all things by his powerful word.

EXAMINE the passages quietly on your own for 5–10 minutes, making observations, taking notes and using colors to highlight words and themes of interest. Then consider these discussion questions.

DISCUSS, in groups of 2–4, your observations of the text and the following questions:

1. What does each passage focus on?

2. What do they tell us about Jesus? About creation?

3. Does reading these passages together give you any different impressions than reading them separately?

4. What do you think it means that "in him all things hold together" (Col 1:17) and the Son is "sustaining all things by his powerful word" (Heb 1:3)? What do these statements suggest about Jesus' current interaction with the world?

SHARE the most significant insights with the larger group.

PRAY as a group. Praise Jesus for creating and sustaining the world.

REFLECT. Each day this week, look for ways that Christ holds all things together. Consider nature around you, the human body, and the stars. What does it mean that Jesus helped create these things and holds them together now? Discuss your thoughts with the group at the beginning of the next meeting.

A Scientist's Reflection

As a chemist, I often think about the bonds that hold molecules together, even in our own bodies. Chemistry is awesome to me. I am even more amazed when I consider who made (and makes!) all of those molecules and bonds, the one who makes "all things hold together" and who sustains "all things by his powerful word"—Jesus! God the Father, Son, and Holy Spirit has made all things and continues to make all things, both living (birds, trees, us) and nonliving (rivers, mountains, and stars).

Recommended Songs

"**You're Beautiful**," by Phil Wickham (2007)

"**Fairest Lord Jesus**," a German hymn with nineteenth century roots

"**Starry Night**," by Chris August (2010)

Further Reading

Proverbs 8:22–31. How does the representation of wisdom in these ten verses compare to the description of Jesus in the three New Testament passages above?

Choose one of the gospel accounts (Matthew, Mark, Luke, or John) and take note of how Jesus interacts with creation.

Mark Harris, "Creation and Christ" and "Creation and the Beginnings of the Idea of God as Trinity," in *The Nature of Creation: Examining the Bible and Science*. (London and New York: Routledge, 2014), 70–81.

CHAPTER 2

The Wonder of Creation

REVIEW LAST SESSION:
Share your thoughts and observations about how Christ holds all things together.

OPENING QUESTION:
If you wrote a song or poem of praise to God, what would you include in it?

The realization that we are not God, coupled with the awareness that God's creation is majestic, should rightly prompt in us a sense of awe. God's creative work is eloquently and poetically described in Psalm 104, an ancient Hebrew song of praise to God.

PRAY as a group that the Holy Spirit would give each of you insight and understanding.

READ this psalm aloud responsively—divide your group in two, with one half reading the odd-numbered verses and the other half reading the even-numbered verses.

Psalm 104:1–32 (NLT)
¹ Let all that I am praise the LORD.
   O LORD my God, how great you are!
   You are robed with honor and majesty.
² You are dressed in a robe of light.
   You stretch out the starry curtain of the heavens;
³ you lay out the rafters of your home in the rain clouds.
   You make the clouds your chariot;
   you ride upon the wings of the wind.

⁴ *The winds are your messengers;*
flames of fire are your servants.

⁵ *You placed the world on its foundation*
so it would never be moved.

⁶ *You clothed the earth with floods of water,*
water that covered even the mountains.

⁷ *At your command, the water fled;*
at the sound of your thunder, it hurried away.

⁸ *Mountains rose and valleys sank*
to the levels you decreed.

⁹ *Then you set a firm boundary for the seas,*
so they would never again cover the earth.

¹⁰ *You make springs pour water into the ravines,*
so streams gush down from the mountains.

¹¹ *They provide water for all the animals,*
and the wild donkeys quench their thirst.

¹² *The birds nest beside the streams*
and sing among the branches of the trees.

¹³ *You send rain on the mountains from your heavenly home,*
and you fill the earth with the fruit of your labor.

¹⁴ *You cause grass to grow for the livestock*
and plants for people to use.
You allow them to produce food from the earth—

¹⁵ *wine to make them glad,*
olive oil to soothe their skin,
and bread to give them strength.

¹⁶ *The trees of the LORD are well cared for—*
the cedars of Lebanon that he planted.

¹⁷ *There the birds make their nests,*
and the storks make their homes in the cypresses.

¹⁸ *High in the mountains live the wild goats,*
and the rocks form a refuge for the hyraxes.

¹⁹ *You made the moon to mark the seasons,*
and the sun knows when to set.

²⁰ *You send the darkness, and it becomes night,*
when all the forest animals prowl about.

²¹ *Then the young lions roar for their prey,*
stalking the food provided by God.

²² *At dawn they slink back*
into their dens to rest.

²³ *Then people go off to their work,*
where they labor until evening.

²⁴ *O LORD, what a variety of things you have made!*
In wisdom you have made them all.
The earth is full of your creatures.

²⁵ *Here is the ocean, vast and wide,*
teeming with life of every kind,
both large and small.

²⁶ *See the ships sailing along,*
and Leviathan, which you made to play in the sea.

²⁷ *They all depend on you*
to give them food as they need it.

²⁸ *When you supply it, they gather it.*
You open your hand to feed them,
and they are richly satisfied.

²⁹ *But if you turn away from them, they panic.*
When you take away their breath,
they die and turn again to dust.

³⁰ *When you give them your breath, life is created,*
and you renew the face of the earth.

³¹ *May the glory of the LORD continue forever!*
The LORD takes pleasure in all he has made!

³² *The earth trembles at his glance;*
the mountains smoke at his touch.

EXAMINE the passage quietly on your own for 5–10 minutes, making observations, taking notes and using colors to highlight words and themes of interest.

DISCUSS, in groups of 2–4, your observations of the text and the following questions:

1. How does this psalm make you feel? How would you want to respond to it?

2. What does the psalm tell us about God, what he has done, and what he is doing?

3. We previously looked at John, Colossians, and Hebrews. What additional perspective does this psalm offer us about creation?

SHARE the most significant insights with the larger group.

PRAY as a group. Praise God for his greatness.

REFLECT. Before the group's next meeting, write your own poem of praise to God. You may find inspiration in style or content from Psalm 8, 19, 33, 74, 98, 104, or 148. Share your poem with the group at the beginning of the next meeting.

A Scientist's Reflection

My awe of God grows the more I study the Bible and the more I study science. I see God's goodness, faithfulness, love, and grace throughout Scripture and throughout creation. I view the world with a sense of gratitude, wonder, and joy. The more I learn, the more curious I am to see how God orders creation and how I am enabled to partner with God in creating new things, such as ideas, molecules, and poems. Here is a poem that I wrote, echoing Psalm 148 from a chemist's perspective:

> Praise the LORD.
>
> Praise the LORD from the classroom,
> praise him in the laboratory, too.
>
> Praise him, all his molecules.
> Praise him, all his proteins and nucleic acids.
>
> Praise him, all alkaloids and steroids.
> Praise him, all you sweet carbohydrates.
>
> Praise him, you manifold terpenoids
> and you polyketides and peptides.

Let them praise the name of the LORD,
for he commanded and they were created.

He formed them from the elements;
he decreed how they should bond.

Praise the LORD from the NMR,*
all you chemists in industry and academia,
whether you be famous or not,
carbon and oxygen, sulfur and nitrogen,
electrons that do all his bonding,

you fluorine and chlorine,
light hydrogen and heavy iodine,

all alkanes and alkenes,
every alkyne and aromatic ring,

all amines and aldehydes,
ketones and carboxylic acids,

esters, amides, and anhydrides,
alcohols and ethers.

Let them praise the name of the LORD,
for his name alone is exalted;
his splendor is revealed in our every molecule.

He has raised up for his people the Christ,
the praise of all his saints,
of the church, the people close to his heart.

Praise the LORD.

(*) *NMR refers to a nuclear magnetic resonance spectrometer.*

Recommended Songs

"**How Great Thou Art**," lyrics by Carl Gustav Boberg (1885)

"**10,000 Reasons (Bless the Lord)**," by Jonas Myrin and Matt Redman (2012)

"**I Could Sing of Your Love Forever**," written by Martin Smith (1995)

"**I Lift My Eyes Up**," by Brian Doerksen (2010)

Further Reading

Ruth Bancewicz, *God in the Lab: How Science Enhances Faith* (Oxford UK and Grand Rapids, MI: Monarch Books, 2015).

Karl W. Giberson, *The Wonder of the Universe: Hints of God in Our Fine-Tuned World* (Downers Grove, IL: IVP Books, 2012).

Deborah Haarsma and Scott Hoezee (editors), *Delight in Creation: Scientists Share Their Work with the Church* (Grand Rapids: Center for Excellence in Preaching, 2012). Individual essays can be accessed through links on this webpage: http://ministrytheorem.calvinseminary.edu/ delight-in-creation/

Dorothy Boorse, "The Wonder of Creation" in *When God and Science Meet: Surprising Discoveries of Agreement* (Washington: National Association of Evangelicals, 2015). Available for downloading through this webpage: http://nae.net/godandscience/.

CHAPTER 3

A Liturgy of Creation

REVIEW LAST SESSION:

Share the poem of praise you wrote from the previous study. Briefly summarize the last two sessions.

OPENING QUESTION:

Think of a story from your family history. What do you find most meaningful about that story?

Genesis 1 is a fascinating story of God creating and giving order to the universe. In radical opposition to other ancient creation stories from Mesopotamia and Egypt (which would likely have been familiar to the early people who first heard this story), the opening chapter of Genesis emphasizes a single God, the goodness of creation, and the special status of humans.

PRAY as a group that the Holy Spirit would give each of you insight and understanding.

READ. Imagine Genesis 1 as though it were composed for a liturgy to be read aloud in a worship service. Select four readers (A–D) to read the following eight parts aloud, as labeled:

A: Introduction (Gen 1:1–2)	**B:** Day 4 (Gen 1:14–19)
B: Day 1 (Gen 1:3–5)	**C:** Day 5 (Gen 1:20–23)
C: Day 2 (Gen 1:6–8)	**D:** Day 6 (Gen 1:24–31)
D: Day 3 (Gen 1:9–13)	**A:** Day 7 (Gen 2:1–4a)[1]

Genesis 1–2:4a (NLT)

A   1:1 *In the beginning God created the heavens and the earth.* 2 *The earth was formless and empty, and darkness covered the deep waters. And the Spirit of God was hovering over the surface of the waters.*

B   3 *Then God said, "Let there be light," and there was light.* 4 *And God saw that the light was good. Then he separated the light from the darkness.* 5 *God called the light "day" and the darkness "night."*

And evening passed and morning came, marking the first day.

C   6 *Then God said, "Let there be a space between the waters, to separate the waters of the heavens from the waters of the earth."* 7 *And that is what happened. God made this space to separate the waters of the earth from the waters of the heavens.* 8 *God called the space "sky."*

And evening passed and morning came, marking the second day.

D   9 *Then God said, "Let the waters beneath the sky flow together into one place, so dry ground may appear." And that is what happened.* 10 *God called the dry ground "land" and the waters "seas." And God saw that it was good.* 11 *Then God said, "Let the land sprout with vegetation—every sort of seed-bearing plant, and trees that grow seed-bearing fruit. These seeds will then produce the kinds of plants and trees from which they came." And that is what happened.* 12 *The land produced vegetation—all sorts of seed-bearing plants, and trees with seed-bearing fruit. Their seeds produced plants and trees of the same kind. And God saw that it was good.*

13 *And evening passed and morning came, marking the third day.*

B   14 *Then God said, "Let lights appear in the sky to separate the day from the night. Let them be signs to mark the seasons, days, and years.* 15 *Let these lights in the sky shine down on the earth." And that is what happened.* 16 *God made two great lights—the larger one to govern the day, and the smaller one to govern the night. He also made the stars.* 17 *God set these lights in the sky to light the earth,* 18 *to govern the day and night, and to separate the light from the darkness. And God saw that it was good.*

19 *And evening passed and morning came, marking the fourth day.*

C   20 *Then God said, "Let the waters swarm with fish and other life. Let the skies be filled with birds of every kind."* 21 *So God created great* sea creatures and every living thing that scurries and swarms in the water, and every sort of bird—each producing offspring of the same kind. And God saw that it was good. ²² Then God blessed them, saying, "Be fruitful and multiply. Let the fish fill the seas, and let the birds multiply on the earth."

²³ And evening passed and morning came, marking the fifth day.

D ²⁴ Then God said, "Let the earth produce every sort of animal, each producing offspring of the same kind—livestock, small animals that scurry along the ground, and wild animals." And that is what happened. ²⁵ God made all sorts of wild animals, livestock, and small animals, each able to produce offspring of the same kind. And God saw that it was good.

²⁶ Then God said, "Let us make human beings in our image, to be like us. They will reign over the fish in the sea, the birds in the sky, the livestock, all the wild animals on the earth, and the small animals that scurry along the ground."

²⁷ So God created human beings in his own image.
In the image of God he created them;
male and female he created them.

²⁸ Then God blessed them and said, "Be fruitful and multiply. Fill the earth and govern it. Reign over the fish in the sea, the birds in the sky, and all the animals that scurry along the ground."

²⁹ Then God said, "Look! I have given you every seed-bearing plant throughout the earth and all the fruit trees for your food. ³⁰ And I have given every green plant as food for all the wild animals, the birds in the sky, and the small animals that scurry along the ground—everything that has life." And that is what happened.

³¹ Then God looked over all he had made, and he saw that it was very good!

And evening passed and morning came, marking the sixth day.

A ²:¹ So the creation of the heavens and the earth and everything in them was completed. ² On the seventh day God had finished his work of creation, so he rested from all his work. ³ And God blessed the seventh day and declared it holy, because it was the day when he rested from all his work of creation.

⁴ This is the account of the creation of the heavens and the earth.

EXAMINE the passage quietly on your own for 5–10 minutes, making observations, taking notes, and using colors to highlight words and themes of interest.

DISCUSS, in groups of 2–4, your observations of the text and the following questions:

1. Which aspects of creation seem most important to you in this story?

2. Genesis 1:2 says the earth was "formless and empty." What is the pattern of bringing form (or order) and fullness to the earth over the first six days?

3. What does this creation account tell you about God and about people? About people's relationship with God?

4. In ancient Babylonian and Assyrian texts, kings are often described as being in the image of gods. What is different in the Genesis 1 use of "the image of God"?

5. This creation story presented a different view of God and people compared to other ancient worldviews. How does Genesis 1 contrast with 21st century worldviews of God, people, and the world?

6. What difference does this Genesis 1 worldview make in your daily life, interactions, and perspectives?

SHARE the most significant insights with the larger group.

PRAY as a group. Praise God for his wonderful creation. Praise God for making it orderly, good, and bountiful. Ask for God's help in guiding people to faithfully govern creation as we are commanded in Genesis 1:28.

REFLECT. God has entrusted us to bring greater order and fullness to the world around us. How can you do that this week? Share what you did with the group at the beginning of the next meeting.

A Scientist's Reflection

As I read Genesis 1, I marvel at God who is a God of order, goodness, and abundance; our world and our universe reflect that reality. At the same time, God entrusts us to bring greater order and fullness to the world. God's call on my life has led me to seek the flourishing of the world through biking to work (rather than driving), encouraging my kids to bike to school, saving water, and designing new "green" (environmentally friendly) chemistry experiments for my students. I aim to be a good and faithful steward of the world in obedience to God and I also hope to inspire others to do the same—and in their own creative ways!

Recommended Songs

"**God of Wonders**," by Marc Byrd and Steve Hindalong (2003)

"**Awesome God (Your Voice)**," by Vicky Beeching (2006)

"**How Great Is Our God**," by Chris Tomlin (2004)

Further Reading

John H. Walton, *The Lost World of Genesis One: Ancient Cosmology and the Origins Debate* (Dowers Grove, IL: IVP Books, 2009).

Johnny V. Miller and John M. Soden, *In the Beginning... We Misunderstood: Interpreting Genesis 1 in Its Original Context* (Grand Rapids: Kregel Publications, 2012).

Tremper Longman III, *How to Read Genesis* (Downers Grove, IL: IVP Books, 2005).

Matt Carter and Halim Suh, *God the Creator: A Gospel Centered Exploration in Genesis* (Nashville, TN: LifeWay Christian Resources, 2015).

CHAPTER 4

A New Creation

REVIEW LAST SESSION:
REVIEW LAST SESSION:
Share ways you have sought to bring order and flourishing to creation. Briefly summarize the last three weeks' sessions.

OPENING QUESTION:

When was a time when everything around you felt right, peaceful, or good?

In Genesis 1, God created the world good. "Good" means suitable for its intended purpose, not perfect or complete. It is amazing that God calls us to participate with him in that good work of creating order out of non-order or chaos (Genesis 1:26, 2:15). Our rebellion, effectively saying we did not need or trust God (in Genesis 3), introduced disorder and sin into the world. This disorder affects us and all of creation, distorting what was once good. Jesus broke the power of sin and triggered the beginning of God's new creation. This new creation has already begun, and we are again invited to participate in it. The fullness of this new heaven and new earth will come one day to replace the current creation. The book of Revelation calls Christians to stand firm in the face of persecution and look forward to the final day when God brings his kingdom to earth and all is set right.

PRAY as a group that the Holy Spirit would give each of you insight and understanding.

READ this passage aloud.

Revelation 21:1–22:5 (NIV)

21:1 *Then I saw "a new heaven and a new earth," for the first heaven and the first earth had passed away, and there was no longer any sea.* 2 *I saw* the Holy City, the new Jerusalem, coming down out of heaven from God, prepared as a bride beautifully dressed for her husband. ³ And I heard a loud voice from the throne saying, "Look! God's dwelling place is now among the people, and he will dwell with them. They will be his people, and God himself will be with them and be their God. ⁴ 'He will wipe every tear from their eyes. There will be no more death' or mourning or crying or pain, for the old order of things has passed away."

⁵ He who was seated on the throne said, "I am making everything new!" Then he said, "Write this down, for these words are trustworthy and true."

⁶ He said to me: "It is done. I am the Alpha and the Omega, the Beginning and the End. To the thirsty I will give water without cost from the spring of the water of life. ⁷ Those who are victorious will inherit all this, and I will be their God and they will be my children. ⁸ But the cowardly, the unbelieving, the vile, the murderers, the sexually immoral, those who practice magic arts, the idolaters and all liars—they will be consigned to the fiery lake of burning sulfur. This is the second death."

⁹ One of the seven angels who had the seven bowls full of the seven last plagues came and said to me, "Come, I will show you the bride, the wife of the Lamb." ¹⁰ And he carried me away in the Spirit to a mountain great and high, and showed me the Holy City, Jerusalem, coming down out of heaven from God. ¹¹ It shone with the glory of God, and its brilliance was like that of a very precious jewel, like a jasper, clear as crystal. ¹² It had a great, high wall with twelve gates, and with twelve angels at the gates. On the gates were written the names of the twelve tribes of Israel. ¹³ There were three gates on the east, three on the north, three on the south and three on the west. ¹⁴ The wall of the city had twelve foundations, and on them were the names of the twelve apostles of the Lamb.

¹⁵ The angel who talked with me had a measuring rod of gold to measure the city, its gates and its walls. ¹⁶ The city was laid out like a square, as long as it was wide. He measured the city with the rod and found it to be 12,000 stadia in length, and as wide and high as it is long. ¹⁷ The angel measured the wall using human measurement, and it was 144 cubits thick. ¹⁸ The wall was made of jasper, and the city of pure gold, as pure as glass. ¹⁹ The foundations of the city walls were decorated with every kind of precious stone. The first foundation was jasper, the second sapphire, the third agate, the fourth emerald, ²⁰ the fifth onyx, the sixth ruby, the seventh chrysolite, the eighth beryl, the ninth topaz, the tenth

turquoise, the eleventh jacinth, and the twelfth amethyst. 21 The twelve gates were twelve pearls, each gate made of a single pearl. The great street of the city was of gold, as pure as transparent glass.

22 I did not see a temple in the city, because the Lord God Almighty and the Lamb are its temple. 23 The city does not need the sun or the moon to shine on it, for the glory of God gives it light, and the Lamb is its lamp. 24 The nations will walk by its light, and the kings of the earth will bring their splendor into it. 25 On no day will its gates ever be shut, for there will be no night there. 26 The glory and honor of the nations will be brought into it. 27 Nothing impure will ever enter it, nor will anyone who does what is shameful or deceitful, but only those whose names are written in the Lamb's book of life.

22:1 Then the angel showed me the river of the water of life, as clear as crystal, flowing from the throne of God and of the Lamb 2 down the middle of the great street of the city. On each side of the river stood the tree of life, bearing twelve crops of fruit, yielding its fruit every month. And the leaves of the tree are for the healing of the nations. 3 No longer will there be any curse. The throne of God and of the Lamb will be in the city, and his servants will serve him. 4 They will see his face, and his name will be on their foreheads. 5 There will be no more night. They will not need the light of a lamp or the light of the sun, for the Lord God will give them light. And they will reign for ever and ever.

EXAMINE the passage quietly on your own for 5–10 minutes, making observations, taking notes and using colors to highlight words and themes of interest.

DISCUSS, in groups of 2–4, your observations of the text and the following questions:

1. How is this new creation created?

2. What is life like in this new creation?

3. What do we learn about God from this account of the new creation?

4. Compare the first creation in Genesis 1–2 with this new creation. How are they similar or different?

5. How do God and his people relate in the new creation?

6. What is attractive to you about living in the new creation?

SHARE the most significant insights with the larger group.

PRAY as a group. Pray in grief over the brokenness of creation, then pray in hopeful joy for Jesus' "making everything new" and for the Holy Spirit's guidance for how to live faithfully now as we wait for the new creation.

REFLECT. Before the group's next meeting, read Isaiah 65:17–25 and Romans 8:18–25. How do these passages point forward to the new creation in Revelation? What part can we play in living lives that bear witness to God's rule and new creation? Discuss your thoughts with the group at the beginning of the next meeting.

A Scientist's Reflection

The promise of God's new creation, begun with Jesus' resurrection and completed in Revelation, gives us hope, courage, and joy for navigating the imperfections and brokenness in our lives and in the world. Science cannot fix the world. People cannot fix the world. Only God can fix the world. So what can we do? We can point people to God's new creation through Jesus, and we can take small steps toward love, justice, and shalom. For me this means sacrificially serving my family, my students, my fellow professors, and my neighbors. I seek to lift up the powerless, to give help to the helpless, and to bring hope to the hopeless.

Recommended Songs

"**All Who Are Thirsty**," by Brenton Brown and Glenn Robertson (1998)

"**You Are Holy (Prince of Peace)**," by Marc Imboden and Tammi Rhoton (1994)

"**How Can I Keep from Singing**," by Robert Lowry (1868)

Further Reading

Michael J. Gorman, *Reading Revelation Responsibly: Uncivil Worship and Witness: Following the Lamb into the New Creation* (Eugene, OR: Wipf and Stock, 2011).

David Wilkinson, *The Message of Creation* (Downers Grove, IL: IVP Books, 2002).

Andy Crouch, *Playing God: Redeeming the Gift of Power* (Downers Grove, IL: IVP Books, 2013).

What does the Bible say about creation?

We have read and discussed accounts of creation from John, Colossians, Hebrews, Proverbs, Psalms, Genesis, and Revelation. These sources offer descriptions and explanations of creation with a rich and wonderful variety, yet they present a unified assertion that God is the author of creation. We have seen Jesus' intimate involvement in creation, the marvelous scope and abundance of God's creation, the order and goodness of creation, and the promise of a new creation where all of creation will be made right and reconciled to God.

What has surprised or intrigued you along the way?

What questions do you have about the Bible and creation?

What has stood out to you from the passages you've studied?

Part Two

What does the Bible say about human origins?

For many Christians, talking about the origins of the universe or the origin of life in general is easier than having conversations about human origins. The topic of human origins feels too personal and is intimately connected with the Genesis 1 concept that human beings were created in the image of God.

What does it mean to be created in the image of God? Does it have anything to do with our physical abilities, our DNA, or when and how humans came to be? Are we defined by where we've come from or by who God has called us to be?

The four Bible studies in this part of the book explore what it means to trust the Bible, what occurs in the Genesis 2 creation account, and what views Christians have about origins and about evolution. As you did for the first part of the book, approach these studies with a humble and gracious posture, ready to look at the Bible with fresh eyes, to listen to others in your group, and to learn something new!

CHAPTER 5

Trusting Scripture

REVIEW LAST SESSION:
Share how you can live a life that bears witness to God's rule and new creation.

OPENING QUESTION:

Who was a person you trusted when you were a child, and what is something that they taught you?

Son puras papas. Me estás tomando el pelo. Perhaps you don't speak Spanish—so what does that mean? A word-for-word translation would be "They are pure potatoes. You are taking me by the hair." A better translation is "That's total nonsense. You're pulling my leg." If we think these Spanish statements are making claims about potatoes or hair, even though those words are used, we are completely missing the point.

Likewise, when we trust the Bible, we are trusting God's word given to his people long ago. None of them spoke English. They spoke Hebrew, Greek, and/or Aramaic. Not only were their languages different from ours, their cultures were very different, too. So we all rely on linguistic and cultural interpretation to hear God's word in Scripture.

The letter of 2 Timothy is from Paul, an early church leader, to another church leader, Timothy. Paul encourages and instructs Timothy as he leads the church in his city. Psalm 119 is an ancient Jewish hymn of thanks to God for giving the Jews his laws which reveal who God is and how to be in right relationship with Him.

PRAY as a group that the Holy Spirit would give each of you insight and understanding.

READ these two passages aloud.

2 Timothy 3:14–17 (NIV)

14 But as for you, continue in what you have learned and have become convinced of, because you know those from whom you learned it, 15 and how from infancy you have known the Holy Scriptures, which are able to make you wise for salvation through faith in Christ Jesus. 16 All Scripture is God-breathed and is useful for teaching, rebuking, correcting and training in righteousness, 17 so that the servant of God may be thoroughly equipped for every good work.

Psalm 119:129–136 (NLT)

129 Your laws are wonderful.
    No wonder I obey them!

130 The teaching of your word gives light,
    so even the simple can understand.

131 I pant with expectation,
    longing for your commands.

132 Come and show me your mercy,
    as you do for all who love your name.

133 Guide my steps by your word,
    so I will not be overcome by evil.

134 Ransom me from the oppression of evil people;
    then I can obey your commandments.

135 Look upon me with love;
    teach me your decrees.

136 Rivers of tears gush from my eyes
    because people disobey your instructions.

EXAMINE the passages quietly on your own for 5–10 minutes, making observations, taking notes and using colors to highlight words and themes of interest.

DISCUSS, in groups of 2–4, your observations of the text and the following questions:

1. Where do these passages say that Scripture comes from?

2. According to the texts, what is the role of Scripture?

3. What is the expected result of trusting Scripture? How is it different from trusting a textbook or a journalist's report?

4. What value, if any, do you see in consulting Christian tradition or Christian community in seeking to understand Scripture?

SHARE the most significant insights with the larger group.

PRAY as a group. Thank God for the gifts of Holy Scripture and the Holy Spirit. Ask God to help us as we seek to follow him with all our heart, soul, mind, and strength. Pray for wisdom to sense the truth of Scripture and to discern the good teachings of those who understand the Bible better than we do.

REFLECT. Consider how you read Scripture. Which parts do you read literally (according to the author's intentions) and which literalistically (intending to convey precise, technical detail)? How does the genre of a Bible book or passage affect your approach to that text? Seek God's wisdom about how God wants you to trust Scripture. Share your reflection with the group at the beginning of the next meeting.

A Scientist's Reflection

We can trust the Bible and the Holy Spirit who inspired its writing because "all Scripture is God-breathed" (2 Timothy 3:16). Biblical scholars urge us to read Scripture *literally*, but not *literalistically*. This is not a new development. The fifth-century Christian writer Augustine of Hippo warned against literalistic readings of Genesis: "The narrative of the inspired writer brings the matter down to the capacity of children"[2] by speaking "in a manner that is accommodated to unlearned readers or hearers."[3] Augustine further warned that holding stubbornly to an interpretation of Scripture that clearly contradicts known facts (scientific or otherwise) would hinder non-believers from trusting Christians or any part of the Bible.[4]

Likewise, the 18th century minister John Wesley emphasized our need to understand the original audience of Genesis: "The inspired penman in this history [Genesis], writing for the Jews first and calculating his narratives for the infant state of the church, describes things by their outward sensible appearances and leaves us, by further discoveries of the divine light, to be led into the understanding of the mysteries couched under them."[5]

Neither Augustine nor Wesley could be accused of compromising with revolutions in liberal theology, geology, or evolutionary biology. These did not develop until the 19th century.

A story does not need to be literalistically true to be historically true (referring to real people and real events). For example, Genesis 2:21–22 says Eve was made by God from Adam's rib or side. Clearly, the author is telling us that Eve is made of the same substance as Adam, which conveys an important truth about the nature and value of women, in contrast to other ancient creation stories. Does the author also intend to tell us the scientific mechanism by which God created woman? Is that his main point? It does not seem so. Conceding that some details of certain passages are not meant to be understood literalistically does not necessitate a sacrifice of historical integrity or truthfulness. Nor does it diminish the central, redemptive work of Jesus as expressed in the Christian faith. By not insisting upon literalistic interpretations of every biblical passage, but rather focusing on the literal meaning, we may actually see more clearly God's main messages to us in the Bible.

So if we should be cautious about reading the Bible literalistically, how do we read it literally, as the author intended? While not always easy, this is very important for us to do. In addition to the clear, over-arching purposes of Scripture, the books of the Bible embody a variety of distinct purposes, contexts, languages, genres, expected audiences, and sets of cultural assumptions. These do not diminish the value of the Bible, but enrich it. Yet we do require the help of knowledgeable biblical scholars to properly understand some of the full details of meaning conveyed in the text of Scripture. This is a case of humbly consulting other Christians (historical and modern) to get the most out of the Bible and to come closer to what God wants to say to us in Scripture.

Finally, it should be noted that our Christian faith rests not only on our individual reading of the Bible, but also on the wisdom of fellow Christian thinkers throughout history, the reasonableness of belief, and our individual or corporate experience of the work of the Holy Spirit.

Recommended Songs

"**In Christ Alone**," by Keith Getty and Stuart Townend (2001)

"**Thy Word**," by Michael W. Smith and Amy Grant (1984)

"**Be Thou My Vision**," traditional Irish attributed to Dallan Forgaill (circa sixth century)

Further Reading

Gordon D. Fee and Douglas Stuart, *Reading the Bible for All Its Worth,* Fourth Edition (Grand Rapids: Zondervan, 2014).

John H. Walton and D. Brent Sandy, *The Lost World of Scripture: Ancient Literary Culture and Biblical Authority,* (Downers Grove, IL: IVP Books, 2013).

James Emery White, *Can We Trust the Bible?* (Downers Grove, IL: IVP, 2010).

Darrell L. Bock, *Can I Trust the Bible?* (Downers Grove, IL: IVP, 2007).

Manfred T. Brauch, *Abusing Scripture: The Consequences of Misreading the Bible,* (Downers Grove, IL: IVP, 2009).

CHAPTER 6

Becoming Human

REVIEW LAST SESSION:
Share your reflections on how you read Scripture. Briefly summarize last session's study.

OPENING QUESTION:

What was one important relationship
to you when you were a child?

Genesis 2 complements Genesis 1 in a similar way that the Gospel of Matthew complements the Gospel of John: conveying a story about related events, but with a very different style and emphasis. Rather than being redundant, each illuminates the other and fleshes out its meaning.

PRAY as a group that the Holy Spirit would give each of you insight and understanding.

READ this passage aloud.

Genesis 2:4b–25 (NLT)

²:⁴ᵇ *When the LORD God made the earth and the heavens, ⁵ neither wild plants nor grains were growing on the earth. For the LORD God had not yet sent rain to water the earth, and there were no people to cultivate the soil. ⁶ Instead, springs came up from the ground and watered all the land. ⁷ Then the LORD God formed the man from the dust of the ground. He breathed the breath of life into the man's nostrils, and the man became a living person.*

⁸ Then the LORD God planted a garden in Eden in the east, and there he placed the man he had made. ⁹ The LORD God made all sorts of trees grow up from the ground—trees that were beautiful and that produced delicious fruit. In the middle of the garden he placed the tree of life and the tree of the knowledge of good and evil.

¹⁰ A river flowed from the land of Eden, watering the garden and then dividing into four branches. ¹¹ The first branch, called the Pishon, flowed around the entire land of Havilah, where gold is found. ¹² The gold of that land is exceptionally pure; aromatic resin and onyx stone are also found there. ¹³ The second branch, called the Gihon, flowed around the entire land of Cush. ¹⁴ The third branch, called the Tigris, flowed east of the land of Asshur. The fourth branch is called the Euphrates.

¹⁵ The LORD God placed the man in the Garden of Eden to tend and watch over it. ¹⁶ But the LORD God warned him, "You may freely eat the fruit of every tree in the garden— ¹⁷ except the tree of the knowledge of good and evil. If you eat its fruit, you are sure to die."

¹⁸ Then the LORD God said, "It is not good for the man to be alone. I will make a helper who is just right for him." ¹⁹ So the LORD God formed from the ground all the wild animals and all the birds of the sky. He brought them to the man to see what he would call them, and the man chose a name for each one. ²⁰ He gave names to all the livestock, all the birds of the sky, and all the wild animals. But still there was no helper just right for him.

²¹ So the LORD God caused the man to fall into a deep sleep. While the man slept, the LORD God took out one of the man's ribs and closed up the opening. ²² Then the LORD God made a woman from the rib, and he brought her to the man.

²³ "At last!" the man exclaimed.

"This one is bone from my bone,
    and flesh from my flesh!
She will be called 'woman,'
    because she was taken from 'man.'"

²⁴ This explains why a man leaves his father and mother and is joined to his wife, and the two are united into one.

²⁵ Now the man and his wife were both naked, but they felt no shame.

EXAMINE the passage quietly on your own for 5–10 minutes, making observations, taking notes and using colors to highlight words and themes of interest.

DISCUSS, in groups of 2–4, your observations of the text and the following questions:

1. What aspects of creation seem most important in this story?

2. How does Genesis 2 compare with Genesis 1? What significance do you find in the differences?

3. What do we learn about God and about people in this passage?

4. What questions does this passage raise for you?

SHARE the most significant insights with the larger group.

PRAY as a group. Thank God for caring for us personally, for the partnership of men and women, and for the gift of marriage.

REFLECT. Before the group's next meeting, read Genesis 3 and reflect on what happens to the relationships of humans to God, to each other, and to creation. How does the mood at the end of Genesis 3 compare to that in Genesis 1 and 2?

A Scientist's Reflection

In Genesis 1, we see that humans are wonderfully made in the image of God. In Genesis 2, we see God's intimacy with humans—making us out of earthly materials (either suddenly or gradually, we are not told), breathing life into us, and providing abundantly for us. There is great beauty in both of these stories. I marvel that the woman comes from the side (rather than, say, the head or the foot) of the man, suggesting that they are to be side-by-side partners in doing God's work.

Biblical scholars have a range of views about Genesis 2. Some see it as symbolic and others see it as historical. Semi-historical and archetypal views have also emerged. These different perspectives have all arisen from a close inspection of Scripture and consideration of its linguistic, literary, and cultural context. An additional issue is how to reconcile the meaning of Genesis 2 with the current scientific consensus that the human population was never less than about 10,000 individuals. The next study will look more closely at some of the views that Christians have about origins.

Recommended Songs

"**All Creatures of Our God and King**," words attributed to Francis of Assisi (circa 1225)

"**Morning Has Broken**," lyrics by Eleanor Farjeon (1931)

"**Beautiful Things**," by Lisa and Michael Gungor (2010)

Further Reading

Matthew Barrett and Ardel B. Caneday, eds. *Four Views on the Historical Adam*, with contributions from Denis O. Lamoureux, John H. Walton, C. John Collins, and William Barrick; and including pastoral reflections from Gregory A. Boyd and Philip G. Ryken, Counterpoints Series (Grand Rapids: Zondervan, 2013).

John H. Walton, *The Lost World of Adam and Eve* (Downers Grove, IL: IVP, 2015).

C. John Collins, *Did Adam and Eve Really Exist?: Who They Were and Why You Should Care* (Wheaton, IL: Crossway, 2011).

Peter Enns, *The Evolution of Adam: What the Bible Does and Doesn't Say about Human Origins* (Grand Rapids: Brazos, 2011).

CHAPTER 7

Considering Origins

REVIEW LAST SESSION:
Share your reflections on Genesis 3. Briefly summarize the last two sessions.

> ## OPENING QUESTION:
> Share about an argument or disagreement you had with someone. How did it affect that relationship?

Some people may tell you that there is only one Christian position on origins, but that is neither historically nor currently true. Origen, Augustine, John Calvin, Galileo, John Wesley, C.S. Lewis, Billy Graham, and other prominent Christians have cautioned against taking a dogmatic stance on origins. Each of the different Bible passages on creation has its own emphasis, and that of Genesis 1–2 is that God is the creator, creation is good, and that God chose to relate with us in a special way. Beyond that, there are different ways Christians interpret scriptural references to origins as well as the related scientific evidence. How important is it that there is Christian consensus on the question of origins?

In his first letter to the church in Corinth, Paul, an early church leader, warns against divisions within the church, or the formation of factions. He urges them to unity and calls them to focus on the centrality of Christ.

PRAY as a group that the Holy Spirit would give each of you insight and understanding.

READ this passage aloud. Imagine the situation in Corinth and also reflect on whether Paul's warning is also needed in your own Christian community.

1 Corinthians 1:9–17 (NIV)

⁹ God is faithful, who has called you into fellowship with his Son, Jesus Christ our Lord.

¹⁰ I appeal to you, brothers and sisters, in the name of our Lord Jesus Christ, that all of you agree with one another in what you say and that there be no divisions among you, but that you be perfectly united in mind and thought. ¹¹ My brothers and sisters, some from Chloe's household have informed me that there are quarrels among you. ¹² What I mean is this: One of you says, "I follow Paul"; another, "I follow Apollos"; another, "I follow Cephas"; still another, "I follow Christ."

¹³ Is Christ divided? Was Paul crucified for you? Were you baptized in the name of Paul? ¹⁴ I thank God that I did not baptize any of you except Crispus and Gaius, ¹⁵ so no one can say that you were baptized in my name. ¹⁶ (Yes, I also baptized the household of Stephanas; beyond that, I don't remember if I baptized anyone else.) ¹⁷ For Christ did not send me to baptize, but to preach the gospel—not with wisdom and eloquence, lest the cross of Christ be emptied of its power.

EXAMINE the passage quietly on your own for 5–10 minutes, making observations, taking notes and using colors to highlight words and themes of interest.

DISCUSS, in groups of 2–4, your observations of the text and the following questions:

1. What seems to have divided the church in Corinth that Paul was writing to?

2. How difficult is it to be "perfectly united in mind and thought" (v 10)? How can we move towards that goal while still respecting each other's intellectual freedom?

3. What specific beliefs about origins (if any) should be central to being a Christian? On what beliefs about origins is it fine for believers to disagree?

4. If you have personally changed views about origins, what caused the change?

5. How can Christians with different positions on origins work together rather than against each other in following Jesus?

SHARE the most significant insights with the larger group.

PRAY as a group for unity and respect among Christians. Ask God to give us humility and to point people to Jesus rather than to our own view of origins. May we never get in the way of someone finding Jesus.

REFLECT. Before the group's next meeting, ask your pastor what beliefs about origins they think are represented in your church. How could you or your pastor promote humble and gracious dialogue about origins that could help build mutual understanding in the church? Share with your pastor some of the things you learned in today's study.

A Scientist's Reflection

The major Christian positions on origins are young-earth creation, progressive creation (also called old-earth creation and largely overlapping with the intelligent design movement), and evolutionary creation. Some Christians object to creation/creationism terms and prefer other labels like directed evolution, planned evolution, or theistic evolution. All of these positions are biblically legitimate and consistent with the historic creeds (Apostles' and Nicene), though their compatibility with the current scientific consensus varies considerably.

Individual Christians may choose their position on origins based on biblical interpretation, scientific support, social pressure, or political commitments. Some may attempt to align biblical information with scientific facts about the natural world (an approach called *concordism*); others do not. Some are comfortable only with minor evolutionary changes over time (sometimes called *micro-evolution*), while others accept larger changes (*macro-evolution*). This guide does not seek to advance a particular perspective. Rather, it seeks to encourage readers with the knowledge that each of the positions has a substantial following (they are summarized in Table 1). The resources listed under Further Reading in this section provide in-depth discussions regarding the strengths and weaknesses of various positions on origins. As you consider the topic, however, be gracious with your Christian brothers and sisters, and do not insist upon consensus with issues like this that are peripheral, and not central, to our shared faith.

TABLE 1. Major Christian positions on origins.[6]

	Young-earth creation (YEC)	Progressive creation (PC)	Evolutionary creation (EC)
Believes God created with a plan and purpose?	yes	yes	yes
Accepted age of the universe?	thousands of years	billions of years	billions of years
Types of biological evolution accepted?	micro-evolution	micro-evolution	both micro- and macro-evolution
Believes God is active in sustaining the universe?	yes	yes	yes
Believes God is active in our lives?	yes	yes	yes
View of Genesis 1–3?	literalistic (concordist)	semi-literalistic (concordist)	literal (non-concordist)
Accepts that Adam and Eve were historical figures?	yes	yes	various positions
Accepts that humans are created in the image of God?	yes	yes	yes
Accepts that sin separates humans from God?	yes	yes	yes
Compatible with contemporary mainstream science?	no	partially	yes

As we engage with others in dialogue about the origins of the universe, of life, of species, and of humans, we would do well to adopt the posture of humility and grace that Augustine recommends: "In matters that are so obscure and far beyond our vision, we find in Holy Scripture passages which can be interpreted in very different ways without prejudice to the faith we have received. In such cases, we should not rush in headlong and so firmly take our stand on one side that, if further progress in the search of truth justly undermines this position, we too fall with it. That would be to battle not for the teaching of Holy Scripture but for our own, wishing its teaching to conform to ours, whereas we ought to wish ours to conform to that of Sacred Scripture."[7] Indeed, Scripture can be faithfully interpreted in different ways regarding issues of origins without jeopardizing any of the core historical Christian beliefs. God is still Father, Son, and Holy Spirit. God is still the creator of all things, however he chooses to do it. And Jesus Christ is still our resurrected Lord and Savior.

Recommended Songs

"**This Is My Father's World**," lyrics by Maltbie D. Babcock (1901)

"**They Will Know We Are Christians by Our Love**," by Peter R. Scholtes (1968)

"**Doxology**," lyrics by Thomas Ken (ca. 1675)

Further Reading

Deborah B. Haarsma and Loren D. Haarsma, *Origins: Christian Perspectives on Creation, Evolution, and Intelligent Design* (Grand Rapids: Faith Alive, 2011).

Gerald Rau, *Mapping the Origins Debate: Six Models of the Beginning of Everything* (Downer's Grove: InterVarsity Press, 2012).

Tim Stafford, *The Adam Quest: Eleven Scientists Explore the Divine Mystery of Human Origins* (Nashville: Nelson Books, 2013).

CHAPTER 8

Starting Conversations

REVIEW LAST SESSION:
Share with the group ideas that you or your pastor had about promoting humble and gracious dialogue about origins with other Christians. Briefly summarize the last three sessions.

OPENING QUESTION:

When you were a child, what questions about science or the world did you have? Were you able to find satisfying answers?

Many people have questions about biological evolution. In Christian circles, there has sometimes been sharp debate and disagreement about how Christianity and evolution relate. No matter what we think about evolution, God loves us and knows us intimately. Psalm 139 declares that the Lord cares for us personally and is powerful, all-knowing, and ever-present. The psalmist marvels at our gradual development as babies in the womb, a wonder that can help us in considering evolution.

PRAY as a group that the Holy Spirit would give each of you insight and understanding.

READ this passage aloud.

> Psalm 139:1–18 (NLT)
> [1] O LORD, you have examined my heart
>   and know everything about me.
>
> [2] You know when I sit down or stand up.
>   You know my thoughts even when I'm far away.

³ You see me when I travel
and when I rest at home.
You know everything I do.

⁴ You know what I am going to say
even before I say it, LORD.

⁵ You go before me and follow me.
You place your hand of blessing on my head.

⁶ Such knowledge is too wonderful for me,
too great for me to understand!

⁷ I can never escape from your Spirit!
I can never get away from your presence!

⁸ If I go up to heaven, you are there;
if I go down to the grave, you are there.

⁹ If I ride the wings of the morning,
if I dwell by the farthest oceans,

¹⁰ even there your hand will guide me,
and your strength will support me.

¹¹ I could ask the darkness to hide me
and the light around me to become night—

¹² but even in darkness I cannot hide from you.
To you the night shines as bright as day.
Darkness and light are the same to you.

¹³ You made all the delicate, inner parts of my body
and knit me together in my mother's womb.

¹⁴ Thank you for making me so wonderfully complex!
Your workmanship is marvelous—how well I know it.

¹⁵ You watched me as I was being formed in utter seclusion,
as I was woven together in the dark of the womb.

¹⁶ You saw me before I was born.
Every day of my life was recorded in your book.
Every moment was laid out
before a single day had passed.

¹⁷ How precious are your thoughts about me, O God.
They cannot be numbered!

¹⁸ *I can't even count them;*
they outnumber the grains of sand!
And when I wake up,
you are still with me!

EXAMINE the passage quietly on your own for 5–10 minutes, making observations, taking notes and using colors to highlight words and themes of interest.

DISCUSS, in groups of 2–4, your observations of the text and the following questions:

1. How does this psalm make you feel? How would you want to respond to it?

2. What does the psalm tell us about God, what he has done, and what he is doing?

3. Note the different perspectives offered in verses 13–14 and 15–16. In the first, God was making the baby in the womb. In the second, God planned and watched the baby's development. How do these complementary perspectives offer insight on how we might think about evolution?

SHARE the most significant insights with the larger group.

PRAY as a group. Pray that God would not allow disagreements about evolution to cause divisions between Christians, nor to discourage people from befriending or becoming Christians.

REFLECT. If you know any Christian biologists, ask them what they think about evolution and how it relates to their faith. Find out if your church has an official position on evolution and ask a pastor or elder how open the church is to members having different views on origins.

A Scientist's Reflection

How should Christians think about evolution? Christians should object to claims about evolution that misuse or overstep scientific evidence to make philosophical or atheistic claims against God. Such statements may say, "If evolution is true, God must not exist." The scientific evidence does not evaluate God's existence one way or the other.

We also need to clarify what evolution is and what it is not. Biological evolution means gradual change in organisms over time, with all of life ultimately derived from common ancestors. It is not a belief that the universe (or even life) came about without God's action. It is neither inherently opposed to Christianity nor allied to it. While evolutionary science can describe how life became wonderfully diverse, it cannot tell us whether God is directing evolution. Indeed, evolution (and science in general) cannot say anything about life's purpose, nor about God, nor about the supernatural. Christians have all sorts of responses to biological evolution: opposition, skepticism, indifference, ignorance, affinity, and acceptance. However, many of these positions are responses to a caricature of evolutionary biology, not to the actual scientific evidence. Christian biologists typically see evolution as part of how God creates. Individual churches have varied responses to evolution. See Table 2 for a summary.

TABLE 2. **Several Christian churches' positions on evolution.**[8]

Churches supporting evolution	Episcopal, Evangelical Lutheran, Greek Orthodox, Presbyterian (PC-USA), Roman Catholic, United Church of Christ, United Methodist
Churches opposing evolution	Assemblies of God, Calvary Chapel, Missouri Synod Lutheran, Seventh-day Adventist, Southern Baptist
Churches with unknown positions	Many nondenominational churches

Few people have a clear idea of the history of Christian responses to evolutionary science. Contrary to popular belief, many Christians have accepted evolution since Darwin's day, with two early examples being Harvard botanist Asa Gray and Anglican priest Charles Kingsley. In 1871, Kingsley wrote, "We knew of old that God was so wise that he could make all things; but, behold, he is so much wiser than even that, that he can make all things make themselves."[9] Here Kingsley suggests that by using evolutionary means to create diverse forms of life, God is a more impressive and awe-inspiring Lord than if separate acts of direct creation were used.

Evangelical theologian Thomas Jay Oord sees evolution as "not a threat to authentic Christian faith and not a threat to biblical authority. ... The Bible tells us how to find abundant life, not the scientific details of how life became abundant."[10]

Christian biologist Jeff Schloss likens the gradual development of species through evolutionary development to the gradual process of God's redemption throughout history—both speak to God's incredible patience and abundant love.

Much of the current opposition to evolution among Christians was triggered by the 1961 publication of Whitcomb and Morris's *The Genesis Flood*—more than a century after Darwin's 1859 publication of *On the Origin of Species* (see the Further Reading list for more information on these titles and others discussed here). This literalistic approach to Scripture and fear that evolution leads to atheism or to an erosion of biblical authority is now championed by Ken Ham, founder of Answers in Genesis and author of *The Lie: Evolution*. BioLogos, on the other hand, is a prominent evangelical Christian group supporting evolution. BioLogos's past president Darrel Falk explains this perspective in his *Coming to Peace with Science*. Although BioLogos and Answers in Genesis have different views about biblical interpretation and science, both are very concerned about effective dialogue within church contexts and with non-Christian audiences. A good documentary film on the Bible and evolution that includes extended statements from both young-earth creation and evolutionary creation perspectives is *From the Dust: Conversations in Creation*.

Recommended Songs

"**Come Thou Fount of Every Blessing**," by Robert Robinson (1757)

"**Who Paints the Skies**," by Stuart Townend (2005)

"**Almighty God**," by Tim Hughes (2007)

Further Reading

Ted Peters and Martinez Hewlett, *Can You Believe in God and Evolution? A Guide for the Perplexed* (Nashville: Abingdon, 2008).

Denis Alexander, *Creation or Evolution: Do We Have to Choose?* Second Edition (Oxford, UK and Grand Rapids, MI: Monarch Books, 2014).

R. J. Berry, ed., *Christians and Evolution: Christian Scholars Change Their Mind* (Oxford, UK: Monarch Books, 2014).

Gary N. Fugle, *Laying Down Arms to Heal the Creation-Evolution Divide* (Eugene, OR: Wipf and Stock, 2015).

Daniel M. Harrell, *Nature's Witness: How Evolution Can Inspire Faith* (Nashville, TN: Abingdon, 2008).

National Academy of Sciences, *Science, Evolution, and Creationism* (Washington, DC: National Academies Press, 2008; available as a free download from www.nap.edu/catalog/11876.html)

What does the Bible say about human origins?

This part of the discussion guide considered trusting Scripture, the Genesis 2 creation account, the need for unity even among people holding different views about origins, and ways to think about evolution. An important point is that honest, faithful Christians have a range of perspectives on how to consider human origins in light of the Bible and with respect to scientific evidence. We can, therefore, freely and earnestly explore questions of science and faith with confidence that our core beliefs are not in jeopardy. As people of faith seeking greater understanding, our posture should be one of grace, humility, and love.

Part Three

What does the Bible say about science?

As the study of nature has developed, Christians have naturally been drawn to study the world around us. Many scientists hope to learn more about God (or God's ways) through exploring God's creation. There is a natural temptation to try and "fit" stories in the Bible with what we observe in nature, lining them up to match. This is called *concordism*. Whether we adopt this concordist approach intentionally or unconsciously, we should ask: is concordism fair to the Bible, and fair to science? Or are we asking each of them to answer questions they do not seek to answer?

CHAPTER 9

The Bible and Science

REVIEW LAST SESSION:

Share with the group what you've learned about faith and evolution from talking with Christian biologists and a pastor or elder from your church.

OPENING QUESTION:

What is a favorite book of yours?
What is its genre (fantasy, poetry, history, etc.),
and why do you like it?

Isaiah was a prophet, a messenger sent from God to call the Jewish people to repent of their sins. Isaiah delivers his message in a poetic form. Job is a book recounting conversations about Job's life, also in a poetic form. In the excerpt included in this session, God is speaking to Job.

PRAY as a group that the Holy Spirit would give each of you insight and understanding.

READ these passages aloud.

Isaiah 40:12, 22–24 (NLT)

12 Who else has held the oceans in his hand?
  Who has measured off the heavens with his fingers?
  Who else knows the weight of the earth
  or has weighed the mountains and hills on a scale?

22 God sits above the circle of the earth.
  The people below seem like grasshoppers to him!
  He spreads out the heavens like a curtain
  and makes his tent from them.

^{23} He judges the great people of the world
  and brings them all to nothing.

^{24} They hardly get started, barely taking root,
  when he blows on them and they wither.
  The wind carries them off like chaff.

Isaiah 41:5 (NLT)
^{5} The lands beyond the sea watch in fear.
  Remote lands tremble and mobilize for war.

Job 38:22–24 (NLT)
^{22} "Have you visited the storehouses of the snow
  or seen the storehouses of hail?

^{23} (I have reserved them as weapons for the time of trouble,
  for the day of battle and war.)

^{24} Where is the path to the source of light?
  Where is the home of the east wind?

EXAMINE the passages quietly on your own for 5–10 minutes, making observations, taking notes and using colors to highlight words and themes of interest.

DISCUSS, in groups of 2–4, your observations of the text and the following questions:

1. What is the message of Isaiah and Job in these texts?
2. How does reading a short, isolated passage (rather than a longer passage in its context) affect your interpretation of the passage?
3. If you read these passages literalistically, what scientific conclusions might you make?
4. How do you think science and the Bible relate to each other?

SHARE the most significant insights with the larger group.

PRAY as a group. Read from Psalm 148 or use your own words to declare God's praise from all parts of creation. Ask the Lord to grant us wisdom from the Bible and knowledge from science. Pray that the Holy Spirit would guide us in using this wisdom and knowledge well, to praise God and to promote flourishing for all people and all of creation.

REFLECT. Before the group's next meeting, take a walk in a natural setting where you will encounter plants, animals, and natural beauty. Carefully examine each of these as you encounter them and marvel at how they bring praise to God and wonder to your eyes.

A Scientist's Reflection

The Bible is primarily concerned with questions of ultimate meaning and purpose, revealing who God is and how we are to relate to him. It is a story of God's relationship with his people and his creation, not a mechanistic explanation of the universe or a science textbook. Scripture affirms that God created and sustains the natural world; Scripture does not tell us how God does all of this. In his 1615 *Letter to the Grand Duchess Christina*, Galileo made famous the notion that the Bible teaches us "how to go to Heaven, not how the heavens go." For example, the Bible does not insist on a geocentric model of the solar system (with the earth in the center), nor does it insist on a heliocentric model (with the sun in the center). Either is compatible with the Bible, regardless of what the individual writers of Scripture believed about it. This is because the authority of God's Word is based on its message to its original audience, not on our modern scientific interpretations of the text. Scripture is not science, nor is science Scripture.

Billy Graham, perhaps the most influential Christian evangelist in the past 65 years, warns us against going to the Bible for science. "I don't think that there's any conflict at all between science today and the Scriptures. I think we have misinterpreted the Scriptures many times and we've tried to make the Scriptures say things that they weren't meant to say, and I think we have made a mistake by thinking the Bible is a scientific book. The Bible is not a book of science. The Bible is a book of Redemption, and of course, I accept the Creation story. I believe that God created man, and whether it came by an evolutionary process and at a certain point He took this person or being and made him a living soul or not, does not change the fact that God did create man . . . whichever way God did it makes no difference as to what man is and man's relationship to God."[11]

As Graham affirms, the Bible at no point focuses on scientific detail. Prominent evangelical theologian J. I. Packer wrote, "It should be remembered . . . that Scripture was given to reveal God, not to address scientific issues in scientific terms. . . . It is not for scientific theories to dictate what Scripture may and may not say, although extra-biblical information will sometimes helpfully expose a misinterpretation of Scripture."[12] A classic example of extra-biblical information informing our interpretation of Scripture is the scientific evidence that the world is a sphere and not flat. Graham and Packer agree that we should not be looking for science in the Bible. We should be looking for God in the Bible. As conservative biblical scholars Johnny Miller and John Soden put it, Genesis "is not revealing the science of creation. Instead it is revealing the Creator of science, albeit in a prescientific way."[13]

Recommended Songs

"**All Creatures of Our God and King**," by Francis of Assisi (circa 1225)

"**Indescribable**," by Laura Story and Jesse Reeves (2004)

"**Let Everything that Has Breath**," by Matt Redman (1998)

Further Reading

Richard F. Carlson and Tremper Longman III, *Science, Creation, and the Bible: Reconciling Rival Theories of Origins* (Downers Grove, IL: IVP, 2010).

John H. Walton, *The Lost World of Genesis One: Ancient Cosmology and the Origins Debate* (Downers Grove, IL: 2009).

Tim Morris and Don Petcher, *Science & Grace: God's Reign in the Natural Sciences* (Wheaton, IL: Crossway, 2006).

CHAPTER 10

Limits of Human Knowledge

REVIEW LAST SESSION:
Share with the group your reflections from your walk in nature last session.

OPENING QUESTION:

When have you encountered something in nature that you didn't understand? How did you feel?

When we think about science and faith, we are often tempted to try and think about the world from God's perspective. While this can be somewhat helpful in seeking a larger view, we should be quick to admit that all of our human descriptions of God and of his purposes are woefully inadequate. Job is a poetic narrative recounting the struggle Job and his friends have comprehending why God allows suffering. This excerpt is from the end of Job where God replies to Job's questions and complaints.

PRAY as a group that the Holy Spirit would give each of you insight and understanding.

READ this passage aloud.

Job 38:1–21 (NLT)

¹ Then the LORD answered Job from the whirlwind:

² "Who is this that questions my wisdom
with such ignorant words?
³ Brace yourself like a man,
because I have some questions for you,
and you must answer them.

⁴ Where were you when I laid the foundations of the earth?
  Tell me, if you know so much.
⁵ Who determined its dimensions
  and stretched out the surveying line?
⁶ What supports its foundations,
  and who laid its cornerstone
⁷ as the morning stars sang together
  and all the angels shouted for joy?

⁸ Who kept the sea inside its boundaries
  as it burst from the womb,
⁹ and as I clothed it with clouds
  and wrapped it in thick darkness?
¹⁰ For I locked it behind barred gates,
  limiting its shores.
¹¹ I said, 'This far and no farther will you come.
  Here your proud waves must stop!'

¹² Have you ever commanded the morning to appear
  and caused the dawn to rise in the east?
¹³ Have you made daylight spread to the ends of the earth,
  to bring an end to the night's wickedness?
¹⁴ As the light approaches,
  the earth takes shape like clay pressed beneath a seal;
  it is robed in brilliant colors.
¹⁵ The light disturbs the wicked
  and stops the arm that is raised in violence.

¹⁶ Have you explored the springs from which the seas come?
  Have you explored their depths?
¹⁷ Do you know where the gates of death are located?
  Have you seen the gates of utter gloom?
¹⁸ Do you realize the extent of the earth?
  Tell me about it if you know!

¹⁹ Where does light come from,
  and where does darkness go?
²⁰ Can you take each to its home?
  Do you know how to get there?

> ^{21} But of course you know all this!
>   For you were born before it was all created,
>   and you are so very experienced!"

EXAMINE the passage quietly on your own for 5–10 minutes, making observations, taking notes and using colors to highlight words and themes of interest.

DISCUSS, in groups of 2–4, your observations of the text and the following questions:

1. Imagine yourself as Job, thousands of years ago. If God spoke these words to you, how would you respond?
2. What does this passage tell us about God and about us?
3. What relevance might this passage have to conversations on creation and on science and faith?

SHARE the most significant insights with the larger group.

PRAY as a group. Confess to God our limited wisdom and ask God to remind us of our dependence on him. Thank God for giving us the ability to explore and study his creation.

REFLECT. Before the group's next meeting, read Job 38–42. Respond to God in prayer.

A Scientist's Reflection

This passage from Job is a helpful corrective against my pride, cautioning me that I cannot fully know Scripture nor science. We should therefore be careful not to try and prove God's activity when we do not have a scientific explanation for something—this is often called a "god-of-the-gaps" argument. For example, Isaac Newton invoked God's regular intervention to explain the orderly movement of the planets in our solar system. When Simon Pierre de Laplace further refined Newton's scientific model without the need to invoke miracles, did that give God a smaller role? If we rely on gaps of scientific knowledge to defend God's existence, then we will necessarily be in constant retreat. But this is really a posture of fear and not of faith. We would be better off recognizing that God could be acting even in ordinary, explainable events. As poet and priest John Donne said in his *Eighty Sermons*, "the ordinary things in Nature would be greater miracles than the extraordinary, which we admire most, if they were done but once…only the daily doing takes off the admiration." If we agree with Donne, having scientific explanations of natural phenomena does not necessarily reduce God's role in them. Indeed, the orderly repetition of them is cause for even more admiration.

However, some people believe that having a scientific explanation for an event implies that God is not involved in it. This is a dangerous conflation of mechanism and purpose, two very different and complementary levels of meaning. For example, the spiritual reality of prayer is not diminished by our observation of concurrent electrochemical processes in the brain. Likewise, a kiss is not fully explained by a scientific description. When a husband and wife kiss, is that act merely a puckering of the lips, an application of force, and a transfer of saliva, carbon dioxide, and bacteria? Surely the couple is experiencing purpose, and not just mechanism, in this moment.

We also should not despair if we have difficulty deciding among multiple legitimate interpretations of Scripture. God is bigger than we are. His ways are not our ways. We need to enlarge our idea of who God is—he's more amazing than we thought, and we're not even capable of grasping that fully!

Recommended Songs

"Immortal, Invisible, God Only Wise," by Walter Chalmers Smith (1876)

"You," by Tim Hughes (2004)

"Blessed Be Your Name," by Beth and Matt Redman (2009)

Further Reading

Tom McLeish, *Faith & Wisdom in Science* (Oxford: Oxford UP, 2014).

Del Ratzsch, *Science & Its Limits: The Natural Sciences in Christian Perspective* (Downers Grove, IL: IVP, 2000).

Katharine Hayhoe and Douglas Hayhoe, "The Competencies and Limitations of Science" in *When God and Science Meet: Surprising Discoveries of Agreement* (Washington: National Association of Evangelicals, 2015; download available at http://nae.net/godandscience/).

CHAPTER 11

Science and Christianity

REVIEW LAST SESSION:
Share your thoughts from reading Job 38–42.

OPENING QUESTION:
When was a time you worked hard on something, only to feel that your effort had been wasted?

Many feel that skepticism is a common trait of scientists. Skepticism is also a prominent feature in the Old Testament book of Ecclesiastes. The Teacher, also called Quoheleth (which could mean "assembler" or "collector"), identifies himself with Solomon because of his legendary wisdom. The Teacher essentially concludes that philosophy and science are "meaningless." He is not the only person to experience moments of frustration in the midst of difficult research!

PRAY as a group that the Holy Spirit would give each of you insight and understanding.

READ this passage aloud.

Ecclesiastes 1 (NLT)
[1] These are the words of the Teacher, King David's son, who ruled in Jerusalem.
[2] "Everything is meaningless," says the Teacher, "completely meaningless!"
[3] What do people get for all their hard work under the sun? [4] Generations come and generations go, but the earth never changes. [5] The sun rises and the sun sets, then hurries around to rise again. [6] The wind blows south, and then turns north. Around and around it goes, blowing in circles.

7 Rivers run into the sea, but the sea is never full. Then the water returns again to the rivers and flows out again to the sea. 8 Everything is wearisome beyond description. No matter how much we see, we are never satisfied. No matter how much we hear, we are not content.

9 History merely repeats itself. It has all been done before. Nothing under the sun is truly new. 10 Sometimes people say, "Here is something new!" But actually it is old; nothing is ever truly new. 11 We don't remember what happened in the past, and in future generations, no one will remember what we are doing now.

12 I, the Teacher, was king of Israel, and I lived in Jerusalem. 13 I devoted myself to search for understanding and to explore by wisdom everything being done under heaven. I soon discovered that God has dealt a tragic existence to the human race. 14 I observed everything going on under the sun, and really, it is all meaningless—like chasing the wind.

15 What is wrong cannot be made right.
   What is missing cannot be recovered.

16 I said to myself, "Look, I am wiser than any of the kings who ruled in Jerusalem before me. I have greater wisdom and knowledge than any of them." 17 So I set out to learn everything from wisdom to madness and folly. But I learned firsthand that pursuing all this is like chasing the wind.

18 The greater my wisdom, the greater my grief.
   To increase knowledge only increases sorrow.

EXAMINE the passage quietly on your own for 5–10 minutes, making observations, taking notes and using colors to highlight words and themes of interest.

DISCUSS, in groups of 2–4, your observations of the text and the following questions:

1. What does the Teacher say about pursuing wisdom and knowledge?

2. Explain how you agree or disagree with the Teacher's sayings.

3. In what ways do you pursue wisdom and knowledge?

4. What do you think the Teacher would say about current scientific pursuits?

SHARE the most significant insights with the larger group.

PRAY as a group. Ask God for support and hope when we feel discouraged. Pray for Christians to love and respect scientists and not to fear science. Pray for scientists to respect and befriend Christians and not to fear Christianity.

REFLECT. Before the group's next meeting, imagine that you see Christianity and science in conflict (whether or not you actually do). How can this perspective affect your theology and your approach to science? How do you think non-Christians view Christianity if they consider it in conflict with science? Perform the same thought experiment by imagining that you see Christianity and science as independent realms. Repeat the experience imagining that you see them as complementary realms. Does thinking about the relationship between science and Christianity in various ways impact the way you see (or want to see) Christianity and science relate? Share your thoughts with the group at your next meeting.

A Scientist's Reflection

Since God created the world and gave us the Bible, both nature and Scripture should be reliable sources of truth with no inherent conflict between the two. However, investigating nature and reading Scripture necessarily involve some level of interpretation (and likely misinterpretation), so we should be careful not to overextend the claims of either. Some truths are more directly addressed in the Bible, and others are found in nature. When we encounter apparent tension between science and Christianity, we should not respond with fear but with an eagerness for dialogue and for enriching our faith with deeper understanding. Historians of science and religion affirm that there has been a strong Christian tradition of deep and respectful engagement between faith and science. The idea that a conflict exists between them has been grossly exaggerated.

A close examination of the philosophical foundations of science and of Christianity reveals them to be remarkably harmonious. For example, scientists and Christians believe that nature is consistent and comprehensible, although not necessarily intuitive (so we need observations and experiments). Both groups concur that studying nature is a good and worthwhile endeavor. These philosophical beliefs cannot be proved scientifically, revealing that some level of faith is foundational to science itself.

TABLE 3. The compatibility of foundational beliefs in science and Christianity.[14]

Beliefs foundational for science	Christian beliefs
We should seek natural causes for events.	There are no nature spirits in inanimate objects.
Nature is consistent.	God is consistent.
The world is rationally understandable.	God made us to understand the world.
We need observation and experiment to understand the world, because our intuition can be wrong.	We need observation and experiment to understand the world, because we are limited.
It is worthwhile to study nature.	It is good to study nature, because God made it and commanded us to be stewards of creation.

The news media commonly present science in conflict with Christianity because it generates flashy headlines. The simplicity of the conflict model is easier for them to sell than other models. However, it is worthwhile for Christians to consider other ways science and Christianity can relate. Some consider them independent and non-overlapping, others see them as one and the same, and yet others view science and Christianity as complementary perspectives on the same reality. Brief but helpful overviews of these different models can be found online[15] and in the Faraday paper, "Models for relating science and religion"[16] by Christian biologist Denis Alexander. The way we relate science and Christianity has implications well beyond our understanding of creation and evolution. It is also relevant to bioethics, neuroscience, and environmental concerns. An accessible and engaging introduction to some of these issues can be found in the *Test of Faith* DVD from the Faraday Institute (available at www.testoffaith.com).

Those who promote a narrative of conflict between Christianity and science often cite Galileo as a tragic victim. Many do not realize that Galileo was a devout Christian and that his dispute with church officials can be largely attributed to his confrontational personality and his lack of compelling astronomical evidence at the time.[17] The Galileo affair was more complex than is often portrayed.

The widespread popularization of the warfare metaphor between faith and science owes much to two deeply flawed yet highly influential books by John Draper, *The Conflict Between Science and Religion* (1874), and A. D. White, *A History of the Warfare of Science with Theology in Christendom* (1896). These two controversialists were critical of religion and argued that conflict between science and religion was inevitable, and that science should win. Historian Mark Noll examines the historical and philosophical errors in White's book and laments their impact in his essay, "Science, Religion, and A. D. White: Seeking Peace in the Warfare Between Science and Theology." Noll is joined in his plea for peace by MIT physicist Ian Hutchinson in his article, "Warfare and Wedlock: Redeeming the Faith-Science Relationship." Both Noll and Hutchinson see science and faith as not only compatible, but mutually enriching.

Recommended Songs

"**Dry Bones**," by Michael Gungor (2010)

"**Beautiful Things**," by Lisa Gungor and Michael Gungor (2010)

"**Praise the Source of Faith and Learning**," by Thomas Troeger (1987)

Further Reading

R. J. Berry, ed., *The Lion Handbook of Science & Christianity* (Oxford: Lion Hudson, 2012).

Allan Chapman, *Slaying the Dragons: Destroying Myths in the History of Science and Faith*, (Oxford: Lion Hudson, 2013).

Ronald L. Numbers, ed., *Galileo Goes to Jail and Other Myths about Science and Religion* (Cambridge: Harvard University Press, 2009).

Mark Noll, "The History of Science and Christianity," in *When God and Science Meet: Surprising Discoveries of Agreement* (Washington: National Association of Evangelicals, 2015). Available for downloading through this webpage: http://nae.net/godandscience.

CHAPTER 12

Christians in Science

REVIEW LAST SESSION:
Share your thoughts from thinking about science and faith from the perspectives of conflict, independence, and complementarity.

OPENING QUESTION:

If you had to pick a career in science, what job would that be?

Psalm 111 is another ancient Jewish hymn of praise to God. It is sometimes called the research scientist's psalm. Verse 2 is prominently displayed at the University of Cambridge, marking the entrances of both the new and old Cavendish Laboratories (in English and Latin, respectively). This world-famous physics department boasts twenty-nine Nobel Prize winners. As you read Psalm 111 and Jesus' words in Mark 12:30, consider how these words from the Bible encourage Christians to explore God's creation as a way of loving God.

PRAY as a group that the Holy Spirit would give each of you insight and understanding.

READ these passages aloud.

Psalm 111 (NLT)

¹ Praise the LORD!
I will thank the LORD with all my heart
as I meet with his godly people.
² How amazing are the deeds of the LORD!
All who delight in him should ponder them.
³ Everything he does reveals his glory and majesty.
His righteousness never fails.

^{4} He causes us to remember his wonderful works.
How gracious and merciful is our LORD!

^{5} He gives food to those who fear him;
he always remembers his covenant.

^{6} He has shown his great power to his people
by giving them the lands of other nations.

^{7} All he does is just and good,
and all his commandments are trustworthy.

^{8} They are forever true,
to be obeyed faithfully and with integrity.

^{9} He has paid a full ransom for his people.
He has guaranteed his covenant with them forever.
What a holy, awe-inspiring name he has!

^{10} Fear of the LORD is the foundation of true wisdom.
All who obey his commandments will grow in wisdom.
Praise him forever!

Mark 12:30 (NIV)

^{30} Love the Lord your God with all your heart and with all your soul and with all your mind and with all your strength.'

EXAMINE the passages quietly on your own for 5–10 minutes, making observations, taking notes and using colors to highlight words and themes of interest.

DISCUSS, in groups of 2–4, your observations of the text and the following questions:

1. What are some examples of deeds or works of God that we should delight in pondering?

2. What does it mean to love God with all your mind?

3. What is your favorite field of science? See what you can learn about some Christians in that field, past or present.

4. Are you—or is a Christian you know—thinking of studying science or becoming a scientist? What factors are influencing that decision? What could help this future scientist flourish in faith?

SHARE the most significant insights with the larger group.

PRAY as a group. Thank God for the many Christians in science. Pray that they may be good witnesses in their scientific communities, giving God glory in their work, and living with hope, joy, integrity, and grace. Pray also that they may contribute to understanding, humility, and a healthy respect for science in their communities of faith.

REFLECT. Find out if there are any scientists at your church. If so, ask them how they integrate faith and science into their lives and into their work.

Browse these three websites for helpful and encouraging resources:

- The American Scientific Affiliation: asa3.org
- Christians in Science: cis.org.uk
- The Emerging Scholars Network: emergingscholars.org

A Scientist's Reflection

Christians pursue science to learn more about God's creation, to give us more inspiration to praise him, to benefit people, to benefit God's world, and to be Jesus' witnesses to other scientists. When Jesus calls us to be his witnesses to the ends of the earth (Acts 1:8), that includes science laboratories. It is true that some scientific fields and institutions are more hostile to Christian faith than others, but we should not respond by running away. We should be more alert and prepared, and prioritize the support of the Christian community. When possible, we should seek out or create such communities within those fields and institutions.

In general, Christians should be represented in any career or hobby whose activities are not inherently unethical or illegal. There will always be ideas, structures, and people that could benefit from Christian perspectives and role models. Our participation in helping all of God's creation to flourish includes science and other areas of study.

If you have ability and interest in science, pray about pursuing a scientific career and seek the advice of other believers you trust. As with any other career, hobby, or pursuit: "Trust in the Lord with all your heart; do not depend on your own understanding. Seek his will in all you do, and he will show you which path to take" (Proverbs 3:5–6 NLT).

Know that you would be in good company. Many of the first scientists were Christians, and many scientists today are believers, too.

Prominent historical scientist-believers include these men and women of renoun:

JOHANNES KEPLER
(astronomer and mathematician, described planetary motion)

ROBERT BOYLE
(chemist and physicist, Boyle's law relates gas pressure and volume)

CAROLUS LINNAEUS
(botanist and zoologist, founded modern biological taxonomy)

LEONHARD EULER
(physicist and mathematician, Euler's number = e = 2.71828...)

ANTOINE AND MARIE LAVOISIER
(chemists, named oxygen and hydrogen)

MICHAEL FARADAY
(chemist and physicist, pioneer of electrochemistry)

CHARLES BABBAGE
(mathematician, invented the first computer)

JAMES CLERK MAXWELL
(physicist, Maxwell's equations of electromagnetism)

GREGOR MENDEL (scientist and friar, father of genetics)

LOUIS PASTEUR
(chemist & microbiologist, discovered vaccination & fermentation)

LORD KELVIN
(physicist, telegraph engineer, absolute zero = 0 Kelvin)

J. J. THOMSON (physicist, discovered the electron)

GEORGE WASHINGTON CARVER
(botanist, promoted alternative crops in the poor South)

GEORGES LEMAÎTRE
(physicist, proposed the Big Bang and an expanding universe)

PERCY JULIAN (chemist, pioneer in medicinal steroid synthesis)

This short list includes just a few examples of present-day scientist-believers:

DENIS ALEXANDER
(Cambridge immunologist, geneticist, and biochemist)

DOROTHY BOORSE (Gordon biologist, studies wetland ecology)

FRANCIS COLLINS
(geneticist, NIH director, former director of Human Genome Project)

GUY CONSOLMAGNO
(astronomical researcher and director of the Vatican Observatory)

KATHARINE HAYHOE
(Texas Tech atmospheric scientist, studies climate change)

ARD LOUIS
(Oxford physicist, studies self-assembly and evolution)

MARIO MOLINA
(UC San Diego chemist and Nobel Laureate, studies the ozone layer)

BILL NEWSOME
(Stanford neuroscientist, leader of national BRAIN initiative)

ROSALIND PICARD
(MIT computer scientist, pioneer of affective computing)

CHARMAINE ROYAL
(Duke geneticist and bioethicist, studies race and genetics)

BOB WHITE (Cambridge geologist, studies volcanic activity)

JENNIFER WISEMAN
(astronomer at NASA with Hubble Space Telescope)

Although fewer scientists are religious compared to the general public, 40% of scientists in the U.S. believe in a personal God who answers prayers, a number that has not changed much since 1916.[18] In a comprehensive 2013 survey of American scientists' religious beliefs, 61% of scientists in the U.S. identify as Protestant or Catholic.[19] Many science PhD students are Christians—it is common for graduate Christian fellowships to be largely composed of students in the sciences, and scientists are well represented in InterVarsity's Emerging Scholars Network (emergingscholars.org). The American Scientific Affiliation (asa3.org), the Canadian Scientific & Christian Affiliation (csca.ca), the UK-based Christians in Science (cis.org.uk), and Society of Ordained Scientists (ordainedscientists.wordpress.com) are strong Christian organizations with memberships totaling more than 3,000 scientists. Personal stories or biographies of scientist-believers can be found in many collections, such as those mentioned under "Scientist Believers" in the Additional Resources listed at the end of this book. Current and potential future scientists should explore the "For Christians in Science" section in the Additional Resources.

Recommended Songs

"**Great Is Thy Faithfulness**," by Thomas Chisholm (1923)

"**Praise the Source of Faith and Learning**," by Thomas Troeger (1987)

"**Shout to the Lord**," by Darlene Zschech (1993)

Further Reading

Tim Stafford, *The Adam Quest: Eleven Scientists Who Held on to a Strong Faith While Wrestling with the Mystery of Human Origins* (Nashville: Thomas Nelson, 2013).

Ruth Bancewicz, ed., *Test of Faith: Spiritual Journeys with Scientists* (Eugene, OR: Wipf & Stock, 2010).

Elaine Howard Ecklund, *Science vs. Religion: What Scientists Really Think* (Oxford and New York: Oxford University Press, 2010).

Christine A. Scheller, "Survey Symposium Inspires Hope for Improved Science/Religion Dialogue," American Association for the Advancement of Science, February 28, 2014 (available online at http://www.aaas.org/news/survey-symposium -inspires-hope-improved-sciencereligion-dialogue).

When God and Science Meet: Surprising Discoveries of Agreement (Washington: National Association of Evangelicals, 2015; download available at http://nae.net/godandscience/).

What does the Bible say about science?

Faith and science both reflect reality. Religion has a more holistic view of the world (for example, who made us and why we are here), while science focuses on details (for example, when and how the earth was formed). Both are important and useful approaches, and sometimes they overlap and inform each other. In this section, we've looked at the Bible and science, Christianity and science, humility, and being a Christian in science. Perhaps the studies have increased your interest in specific science-faith topics. If so, explore them further or discuss them with friends or family.

CLOSING REMARKS

Reflections

From David A. Vosburg, PhD, Chemistry Professor

My navigation of science and faith has changed a lot over the years. At first I kept the two separate out of fear. I gradually opened up to exploring science and faith personally once I found role models whose faith looked like mine and whose scientific integrity I trusted. My eyes were opened to new perspectives, I found joy in the journey, and I eventually became professionally engaged in helping others integrate a robust Christian faith and sound science. My goal is not to convince others to adopt my position, but to have respectful dialogue that honors Scripture and takes science seriously. I am deeply grateful for how God has blessed Kate and me along the way, as well as Ellen, Sam, and other colleagues and students. May God bless you, too.

From Kate Vosburg, Pastor

In studying Scripture and combatting my biases against science based on fear, I've realized how much more Scripture tells me about God and the world and how much less it tells me about science. I've come to trust Scripture much more deeply and become less defensive and nervous when people raise questions or issues. For example, I used to read Genesis 1 and be disturbed by conflicting scientific creation accounts. Now when I read Genesis 1, I see a beautiful poetic description of God's creating. I see how the Lord is shown to be good, powerful, and creative. I see the incredible relationship God established with humanity. And it leads me to worship.

I've also come to appreciate science more and marvel at the complexity of the world, which gives me insight into the creative, powerful God whom I serve. For example, at a recent lecture on genetics,

I found myself in awe of God as I listened to the description of human, chimpanzee, and gorilla DNA. Such lectures used to produce anxiety. Now they are places to worship God. May Christ continue to lead you deeper into worship as you learn of the Lord through Scripture and science.

Notes

1. This method of reading Genesis 1 is inspired by Christopher R. Smith, *Genesis* (Colorado Springs: Biblica, 2010), pp. 15-18.

2. Augustine, *St. Augustine: The Literal Meaning of Genesis*, Vol. 1, trans. John Hammond Taylor, S.J., Ancient Christian Writers, no. 41 (New York: Newman Press, 1982), p. 54.

3. Ibid., pp. 35–36.

4. Ibid., pp. 42–43. See also Alister McGrath, "Augustine's Origin of Species," *Christianity Today* (5 August 2009).

5. John Wesley, *Wesley's Notes on the Bible* (Grand Rapids: Francis Asbury Press, 1987), p. 25.

6. For more detailed comparisons of these and other positions on origins, see (a) Deborah B. Haarsma and Loren D. Haarsma, *Origins: Christian Perspectives on Creation, Evolution, and Intelligent Design* (Grand Rapids: Faith Alive, 2011), pp. 299–302; (b) Gerald Rau, *Mapping the Origins Debate: Six Models of the Beginning of Everything* (Downer's Grove: IVP, 2012), pp. 41, 194–205; and (c) Denis O. Lamoureux, *Evolution: Scripture and Nature Say Yes!* (Grand Rapids: Zondervan, 2016), pp. 113–133.

7. Augustine, *The Literal Meaning of Genesis* (Hyde Park, NY: New York Press, 2002), cited in Alister E. McGrath, *The Foundations of Dialogue in Science and Religion* (Oxford: Blackwell, 1998), p. 119.

8. Joel W. Martin, *The Prism and the Rainbow: A Christian Explains Why Evolution is Not a Threat* (Baltimore: Johns Hopkins University Press, 2010).

9. Charles Kingsley, "The Natural Theology of the Future," read at Sion College January 10, 1871 (online: http://www.online-literature.com/charles-kingsley/scientific/7/).

10. Thomas Jay Oord, "Evangelicals Accept Evolution," November 15, 2010 (online: http://thomasjayoord.com/index.php/blog /archives/evangelicals_accept_evolution).

11. *Billy Graham: Personal Thoughts of a Public Man* (Colorado Springs: Cook Communications, 1997) pp. 72–74. Taken from the transcript of an interview of Graham by David Frost on BBC-2 in 1964.

12. J. I. Packer, *God Has Spoken: Revelation and the Bible*, 3rd ed. (Grand Rapids: Baker, 1993), pp. 167–168.

13. Johnny V. Miller and John M. Soden, *In the Beginning . . . We Misunderstood: Interpreting Genesis 1 in Its Original Context* (Grand Rapids: Kregel, 2012), p. 40.

14. Haarsma and Haarsma, *Origins*, p. 43.

15. BioLogos, "Are Science and Christianity at War?" updated June 27, 2012 (online: http://biologos.org/questions/science-and-religion).

16. Denis R. Alexander, "Models for Relating Science and Religion," *Faraday Papers* no. 3 (2007) (online: www.faraday.st-edmunds .cam.ac.uk/resources/Faraday%20Papers/Faraday%20Paper%20 3%20Alexander_EN.pdf).

17. Maurice A. Finocchiaro, "That Galileo Was Imprisoned and Tortured for Advocating Copernicanism," in *Galileo Goes to Jail and other Myths about Science and Religion*, ed. Ronald L. Numbers (Cambridge: Harvard University Press, 2009), pp. 68–78.

18. Edward J. Larson and Larry Witham, "Scientists are still keeping the faith," *Nature* 1997, 386, 435–436.

19. Elaine Howard Ecklund and Christopher Scheitle, "Religious Communities, Science, Scientists, and Perceptions: A Comprehensive Survey," presented to the AAAS on February 16, 2014 (online: www.aaas.org/sites/default/files/content_files/RU_ AAASPresentationNotes_2014_0219 (1).pdf).

Additional Resources

This section combines the "Further Reading" suggestions from the chapters with additional resources for exploring relevant topics more deeply. Multiple Christian perspectives are represented: young-earth creation (YEC), progressive creation (PC), and evolutionary creation (EC). The intelligent design (ID) content that is included generally adopts a PC perspective.

Comparisons of Views on Origins

Barrett, Matthew, and Ardel B. Caneday, eds. *Four Views on the Historical Adam*. Grand Rapids: Zondervan, 2013. Proponents of evolutionary creation (Denis Lamoureux), archetypal creation (John Walton), old-earth creation (C. John Collins), and young-earth creation (William Barrick) present their positions and critique each others' views. Two pastoral reflections are offered by Gregory Boyd and Philip Ryken.

Haarsma, Deborah and Loren. *Origins: Christian Perspectives on Creation, Evolution, and Intelligent Design*. 2nd ed. Grand Rapids: Faith Alive, 2011. An engaging, gracious, and informative guide on theological and scientific aspects of origins. The second edition is balanced and ideal for a broad Christian audience.

Rau, Gerald. *Mapping the Origins Debate: Six Models of the Beginning of Everything*. Downer's Grove, IL: IVP, 2012. An even-handed treatment of philosophical, scientific, and theological assumptions and implications of six views of origins: naturalistic evolution, nonteleological evolution, planned evolution, directed evolution, old-earth creation, and young-earth creation.

Creation in the Bible

Brown, William. *Seven Pillars of Creation*. New York: Oxford, 2010. Examines seven traditions or ways of creation in the Old Testament: Genesis 1:1–2:3, Genesis 2:4b–3:24, Job 38–41, Psalm 104, Proverbs 8:22–31, Ecclesiastes 1:2–11 and 12:1–7, and Isaiah 40–55. Each offers a valuable perspective, combining to give us a healthy and balanced view of creation from Scripture.

Carlson, Richard, and Tremper Longman III. *Science, Creation, and the Bible: Reconciling Rival Theories of Origins*. Downers Grove, IL: InterVarsity 2010. An examination of theological, scientific, and biblical aspects of creation. This book discusses both Old and New Testament passages relevant to creation.

Enns, Peter. *The Evolution of Adam: What the Bible Does and Doesn't Say about Human Origins*. Grand Rapids: Brazos, 2012. This book holds that evolutionary science precludes a historical Adam. From an incarnational view of Scripture, the author aims to reconcile the Bible and evolution.

Harris, Mark. *The Nature of Creation: Examining the Bible and Science*. New York: Routledge, 2014. A Trinitarian investigation of creation texts in the Old and New Testaments and their relation to modern science, with an aim to re-inform us and to re-align Scripture and science.

Wilkinson, David. *The Message of Creation*. Downers Grove, IL: InterVarsity 2002. An exploration of themes of creation through 20 different biblical passages from Genesis to Revelation. Includes a study guide and an appendix on reconciling Scripture with science.

Reading Genesis

Collins, C. John. *Did Adam and Eve Really Exist?: Who They Were and Why You Should Care* (Wheaton, IL: Crossway, 2011). Scholarly yet humble defense of the historicity of Adam and Eve using both biblical and extra-biblical sources. Offers a balanced assessment of what we do and do not know about Adam and Eve and several possible historical scenarios.

Longman, Tremper III. *How to Read Genesis.* Downers Grove, IL: IVP, 2005. Strategies for reading Genesis as literature, in its own world, as God's story, and in relationship to Jesus Christ.

Miller, Johnny, and John Soden. *In the Beginning . . . We Misunderstood: Interpreting Genesis 1 in Its Original Context.* Grand Rapids: Kregel, 2012. Two evangelical biblical scholars ask what Genesis meant to the original author and original readers. They conclude that the text of Genesis 1 and the context of ancient Israel provide reasons to believe that Genesis 1 was not intended to teach a scientific view of creation.

Walton, John H. *The Lost World of Adam and Eve: Genesis 2–3 and the Human Origins Debate.* Downers Grove, IL: IVP, 2015. Adam and Eve are viewed as real, historical people, yet treated in the text mainly as archetypes for all humans. They may or may not have been the first humans; God gave them a priestly responsibility to tend sacred space. Again drawing from evidence in the Ancient Near East, the text is seen as not being in conflict with modern science. Also included is a discussion by N.T. Wright on Paul's use of Adam in the New Testament.

———. *The Lost World of Genesis One.* Downers Grove, IL: IVP, 2009. Understanding Genesis 1 through the eyes of ancient Israelites liberates the text from conflict with science. The story emphasizes functional origins rather than material origins, with all creation intended as a cosmic temple to glorify God. Humans are given a special, priestly role in this temple.

Reading the Bible

Brauch, Manfred T. *Abusing Scripture: The Consequences of Misreading the Bible.* Downers Grove, IL: IVP, 2009. An accessible, helpful, and practical corrective from the temptation to distort Scripture to fit our own preconceived views.

Fee, Gordon D., and Douglas Stuart. *Reading the Bible for All Its Worth.* 4th ed. Grand Rapids: Zondervan, 2014. A popular guide for understanding biblical genres, translations, and interpretations. Includes helpful reading tips and focuses on applying the Bible to your life.

Walton, John H., and D. Brent Sandy. *The Lost World of Scripture: Ancient Literary Culture and Biblical Authority*. Downers Grove, IL: IVP, 2013. Old and New Testament scholars offer important insights on the oral tradition, cultural context, authority, and interpretation of the Bible.

White, James Emery. *Can We Trust the Bible?* Downers Grove, IL: IVP, 2010. A short booklet with responses to common questions about the veracity of Scripture.

Scientist Believers

Bancewicz, Ruth. *God in the Lab: How Science Enhances Faith*. Grand Rapids: Monarch, 2015. An exploration of themes (creativity, imagination, beauty, wonder, and awe) alongside scientists' personal stories in which science enhances faith.

———, ed. *Test of Faith: Spiritual Journeys with Scientists*. Eugene, OR: Wipf & Stock, 2010. Ten scientists share their life stories and their reflections on faith and science. This volume complements the film *Test of Faith* (see below) and features many of the same scientists.

Berry, R. J., ed. *True Scientists, True Faith*. Grand Rapids: Monarch, 2014. Twenty prominent scientists describe the intersection of their science and their personal faith. Biology, geology, chemistry, physics, and astronomy are among the fields represented.

Ecklund, Elaine Howard. *Science vs. Religion: What Scientists Really Think*. New York: Oxford University Press, 2010. A landmark sociological study on the views of religion and spirituality held by 1,700 natural and social scientists from top research universities. Survey data dispel the common assumption that most scientists are hostile to religion. Personal interviews with 275 scientists add depth to the narrative.

Haarsma, Deborah, and Scott Hoezee, eds. *Delight in Creation: Scientists Share Their Work with the Church*. Grand Rapids: Center for Excellence in Preaching, 2012. Several scientists and a historian describe the delight they find in their areas of expertise as it relates to their wonder at God's creation. Online: http://ministrytheorem.calvinseminary.edu/delight-in-creation/.

Stafford, Tim. *The Adam Quest: Eleven Scientists Explore the Divine Mystery of Human Origins.* Nashville: Nelson Books, 2013. Stafford interviews and narrates the journeys and views of 11 American and British scientists (all Christians) with a range of perspectives on human origins.

History of Science and Christianity

Berry, R. J., ed. *The Lion Handbook of Science & Christianity.* Oxford: Lion Hudson, 2012. Beautifully illustrated guidebook with expert treatment of a wide range of topics. Excellent overview.

Chapman, Allan. *Slaying the Dragons: Destroying Myths in the History of Science and Faith.* Oxford: Lion Hudson, 2013. An enjoyable and informative defense of Christianity against New Atheist claims and popular myths about science and religion.

Hannam, James. *The Genesis of Science: How the Christian Middle Ages Launched the Scientific Revolution.* Washington, DC: Regnery, 2011. A historical account of scientific developments in the Middle Ages that refutes the common view of medieval ignorance and barbarism.

Numbers, Ronald, ed. *Galileo Goes to Jail and Other Myths about Science and Religion.* Cambridge: Harvard University Press, 2010. Contributions from 25 scholars (only a few of whom are religious believers) debunk prevalent misconceptions about science and religion, setting the historical record straight.

Christian Perspectives: Opposing Biological Evolution

Behe, Michael. *Darwin's Black Box: The Biochemical Challenge to Evolution.* New York: Free Press, 2006. A key book of the Intelligent Design movement, first published in 1998. The concept of irreducible complexity is offered as a test for whether gradual Darwinistic evolution is plausible for a given system.

Ham, Ken. *The Lie: Evolution.* Green Forest, AR: Master Press, 2012. Presents a young-earth creation perspective and asserts that beliefs in evolution and in an old earth are driving people away from Christian belief and the authority and accuracy of the Bible.

MacArthur, John. *The Battle for the Beginning*. Nashville: Thomas Nelson, 2005. A popular pastor defends a literalistic six-day creation account from Genesis 1–3. He argues against naturalism and the old-earth creation perspective of Hugh Ross and the Reasons to Believe organization.

Meyer, Stephen. *Signature in the Cell: DNA and the Evidence for Intelligent Design*. New York: HarperOne, 2009. A discussion of the complexity of cells and an argument that chemical evolution, chance, and chemical necessity are not sufficient to explain the emergence of life. This is taken as evidence for intelligent design.

Rana, Fazale, and Hugh Ross. *Who Was Adam? A Creation Model Approach to the Origin of Humanity*. Covina, CA: Reasons to Believe, 2015. An old-earth creation perspective on human origins, looking at both scientific evidence and biblical explanations.

Christian Perspectives: Supporting Biological Evolution

Alexander, Denis. *Creation or Evolution: Do We Have to Choose?* 2nd ed. Grand Rapids: Monarch, 2014. A thorough and careful exploration of what creation and evolution mean, how they can be resolved, and several viable options for understanding Adam and Eve.

Falk, Darrel. *Coming to Peace with Science*. Downers Grove, IL: IVP, 2004. A scientifically clear and personal look at evolution and faith by an evangelical Christian and biologist. A clear call for peace between science and faith and between believers with different views about creation.

Fugle, Gary. *Laying Down Arms to Heal the Creation-Evolution Divide*. Eugene, OR: Wipf & Stock, 2015. A hopeful treatment of evolutionary biology and Christian faith. Mutual respect among biologists and Christians may actually help the core beliefs of biology and Christianity gain acceptance in society.

Giberson, Karl, and Francis Collins. *The Language of Science and Faith*. Downers Grove, IL: IVP, 2011. Clear responses to common questions about evolution, the Bible, and creation in a way that honors Scripture and science and seeks to find a harmony between them.

Harrell, Daniel. *Nature's Witness: How Evolution Can Inspire Faith.*
Nashville: Abingdon, 2010. A personable, pastorly, and accessible
treatment of important questions alongside the author, his friend
Dave, and Aunt Bernice. Chapter 6 is written as a prayer to God.

Discussion Guides

Baker, Catherine. *The Evolution Dialogues: Science, Christianity, and the
Quest for Understanding.* Washington, DC: AAAS, 2006. A balanced and thoughtful guide on evolutionary science and Christianity with an interwoven story of a Christian undergraduate
struggling to reconcile evolutionary biology with her faith.

Bock, Darrell L. *Can I Trust the Bible?* Downers Grove, IL: IVP, 2007. A
six-week discussion guide focusing on New Testament passages,
the origins of the Bible, and the reliability of Scripture.

Carner, Matt, and Halim Suh. *God the Creator: A Gospel-Centered Exploration in Genesis.* Nashville: LifeWay, 2015. A six-week study
guide that connects New Testament themes with Genesis 1–11.

Stroble, Paul. *What About Religion & Science? A Study of Reason and
Faith.* Nashville: Abingdon, 2007. A seven-week study guide
designed for adults in Sunday school, small group, or retreat
settings.

Films for Discussions

*The Author of Life: Making Connections between Faith and Biology
through Film* (9ᵗʰ Avenue Studios 2014). Seven short films (4–7
minutes each) designed for Christian high school students by a
chaplain and a biology teacher. The episodes are: "Seeing Things
Differently," "The Creation Story," "God as Artist," "God's Creative Process," "How Our Creator Shapes Us," "Image of God,"
and "Caring for Creation." Features students, flora, and fauna of
Hawaii. Online: theauthoroflife.org.

From the Dust: Conversations in Creation (Highway Media 2012). Four
11- to 25-minute segments (67 minutes total) with personal
stories and strong theological content focused on Genesis,
creation, and evolution. This film is great for starting discussions

and juxtaposes both YEC and EC views. Features N. T. Wright, John Walton, John Polkinghorne, Alister McGrath, Ard Louis, Peter Enns, Jeff Schloss, Rick Colling, Answers in Genesis, and Canopy Ministries. A free discussion guide is available. Online: fromthedustmovie.org.

Origins: A Six-Session Investigation of Creation, Evolution, and Intelligent Design (Faith Alive 2014). Six 9- to 14-minute videos with Deborah and Loren Haarsma. May be used to supplement their *Origins* book or as a stand-alone resource. The six sessions are: "It's Not Science Versus God," "It's Not Science Versus Scripture," "Genesis and Geology," "Astronomy and the Big Bang," "Evolution," and "Human Origins and Adam and Eve." Online: http://origins.faithaliveresources.org/#watch_online. A discussion guide is also available.

Origins Today: Genesis through Ancient Eyes (REi Media 2012). Biblical teaching from John Walton, aimed at church or youth groups. 127 minutes. Bonus material includes interviews by VeggieTales creator Phil Vischer and personal testimonies from John Walton. Online: vimeo.com/66282642.

Our Fascinating Universe: A Journey Through God's Creation (Vision Video 2012). Focuses on astronomy and cosmology, featuring Alister McGrath, John Lennox, and four German/Swiss scientists. Has 35- and 55-minute versions and 40 minutes of bonus material.

Our Father's World (Vision Video 2012). A 27-minute video exploring the biblical mandate to care for creation. Features evangelical leaders and scholars Joel Hunter, Bill and Lynne Hybels, Tony Campolo, James Merritt, and Mark Liederbach. Online: ourfathersworldfilm.com.

Religion and Science: Pathways to Truth (Wesley Ministry Network 2008). Nine 26- to 32-minute videos with Francis Collins, David Wilkinson, Darrel Falk, John Polkinghorne, Beth Norcross, and other scientists and theologians. Aimed at adult Sunday school classes. Covers biblical, theological, historical, philosophical, ethical, and eschatological topics. Bonus material includes Nobel laureates William Phillips and Charles Townes. A leader's guide is also available.

BioLogos (EC): Founded by geneticist Francis Collins and now led by astronomer Deborah Haarsma, BioLogos sees harmony between science and biblical faith in an evolutionary understanding of God's creation (online: www.biologos.org).

Discovery Institute, Center for Science and Culture (ID): Philosopher of science Stephen Meyer heads the Discovery Institute's Center for Science and Culture. The center looks for scientific evidence that nature is the result of intelligent design and opposes evolutionary explanations (online: www.discovery.org/id/).

Reasons to Believe (PC): Astrophysicist Hugh Ross is founder and president of Reasons to Believe. This organization focuses on apologetics and a concordist interpretation of science and the Bible (online: www.reasons.org).

Other Resources

Applegate, Kathryn, and J. B. Stump, eds. *How I Changed My Mind About Evolution: Evangelicals Reflect on Faith and Science*. Downers Grove, IL: IVP, 2016. Personal stories of pastors, theologians, philosophers, and scientists (mainly from the United States) and their changing views on biological evolution and its relationship to Christian faith.

Berry, R. J., ed. *Christians and Evolution: Christian Scholars Change Their Mind*. Oxford: Monarch Books, 2014. Personal stories of Christian scholars, mainly scientists, and their changing views on biological evolution.

Crouch, Andy. *Playing God: Redeeming the Gift of Power*. Downers Grove, IL: IVP, 2013. A hopeful exploration of how the power of individuals and institutions can be stewarded to promote human flourishing.

Cunningham, Mary Kathleen, ed. *God and Evolution: A Reader*. New York: Routledge, 2007. A collection of writings from past and present scientists, theologians, and philosophers spanning a wide range of views (including atheists) on God and evolution.

Fleming, Fraser. *The Truth About Science and Religion: From the Big Bang to Neuroscience*. Eugene, OR: Wipf and Stock, 2016. A Christian chemist presents a clear account of the interaction of Christianity with science and the development of science. Each chapter has helpful discussion questions and an annotated bibliography.

Giberson, Karl W. *The Wonder of the Universe: Hints of God in Our Fine-Tuned World*. Downers Grove, IL: IVP, 2012. A colorful exploration of the science, scientists, and history that relate to the fine-tuning of our universe and hints of a creator God.

Godfrey, Stephen J., and Christopher R. Smith. *Paradigms on Pilgrimage: Creationism, Paleontology, and Biblical Interpretation*. Jacksonville, FL: Clements, 2005. A museum paleontologist and a biblical scholar reflect on the fossil and scriptural evidence, respectively, that led to their personal journeys of understanding biblical creation.

Gorman, Michael J. *Reading Revelation Responsibly: Uncivil Worship and Witness: Following the Lamb into the New Creation*. Eugene, OR: Wipf and Stock, 2011. A grounded, balanced, and reflective guide to reading Revelation with helpful discussion questions throughout.

McLeish, Tom. *Faith & Wisdom in Science*. New York: Oxford University Press, 2014. A British physicist develops a theology of science inspired by biblical wisdom and especially Job 38–42. He offers Christians suggestions for relating science to current societal challenges.

Miller, Kenneth R. *Only a Theory: Evolution and the Battle for America's Soul*. New York: Viking, 2008. A Catholic, Brown University biologist defends biological evolution and its compatibility with Christian faith while critiquing the Intelligent Design movement.

Morris, Tim, and Don Petcher. *Science & Grace: God's Reign in the Natural Sciences*. Wheaton, IL: Crossway, 2006. A Trinitarian view of Christianity and science through a lens of grace.

National Academy of Sciences. *Science, Evolution, and Creationism*. Washington, DC: National Academies Press, 2008. (online: www.nap.edu/catalog/11876.html). A colorful and accessible description of biological evolution and its potential compatibility with various faith traditions.

National Association of Evangelicals. *When God and Science Meet: Surprising Discoveries of Agreement.* Washington: National Association of Evangelicals, 2015. (online: http://nae.net/godandscience/). A collection of short, positive essays by evangelical scientists, pastors, theologians, and educators expressing positive relationships between a robust Christian faith and several scientific topics.

Peters, Ted and Martinez Hewlett. *Can You Believe in God and Evolution? A Guide for the Perplexed.* Nashville: Abingdon, 2008. A theologian and a biologist explore biological evolution and various views on God, evolution, and divine action.

Ratzsch, Del. *Science & Its Limits: The Natural Sciences in Christian Perspective.* Downers Grove, IL: IVP, 2000. A Christian philosopher describes the nature of science, what it can (and cannot) tell us, what challenges it presents to Christian faith, and how Christians should respond.

Venema, Dennis R., and Scot McKnight. *Adam and the Genome: Reading Scripture after Genetic Science.* Grand Rapids: Brazos, 2017. A Christian geneticist and a New Testament scholar team up to offer insights on evolution, genetics, and the historical Adam.

About the Authors

David A. Vosburg is a Professor of Chemistry at Harvey Mudd College in Claremont, California. He has a Ph.D. in chemistry from The Scripps Research Institute and was a post-doctoral fellow at Harvard Medical School. He is a Fellow of the American Scientific Affiliation, a Henry Dreyfus Teacher-Scholar, and an Associate of the Faraday Institute for Science and Religion. He has partnered with InterVarsity Christian Fellowship (IVCF) since 1993.

Kate Vosburg has been a campus minister with IVCF since 1999 and holds a Master of Arts in Theology from Fuller Theological Seminary. David, Kate, and their three children live in Upland, California and enjoy storytelling, board games, and building castles.

Also Available
from Pier Press

Pier Press®

Walk with the Gospel Writers:
Personal Journals for Spiritual Discovery

Discover biblical truths for yourself.
These journals provide an opportunity for you
to blend attentive reading with rumination, contemplation,
and listening for the Spirit of God.

Available in handsome wire-bound editions or in a print-your-own
.PDF version. Visit PierPress.com for more information.

CPSIA information can be obtained
at www.ICGtesting.com
Printed in the USA
FSHW01n1431220518
48486FS